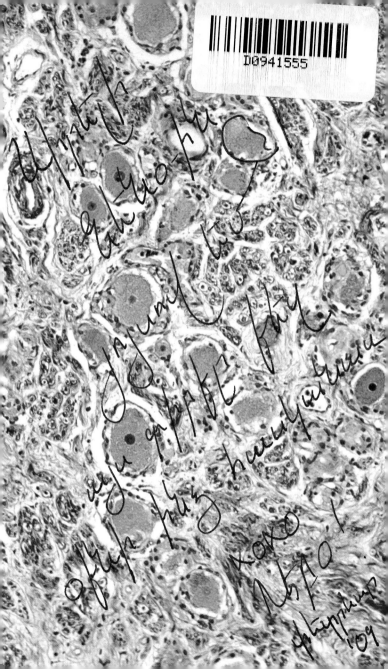

BRAIN
IN YOUR
POCKET

OVER 3,000 ESSENTIAL FACTS

CHRISTOPHER M. STRANGE

This Modern Books Edition published in 2008 by Elwin Street Ltd.

Conceived and produced by
Elwin Street Limited
144 Liverpool Road
London N1 1LA, UK
www.elwinstreet.com

Cover design: Sharanjit Dhol
Layout design: Ian Hunt

ISBN: 978-0-9556421-6-6

Printed in China

Contents

STRUCTURE
AND
FUNCTION

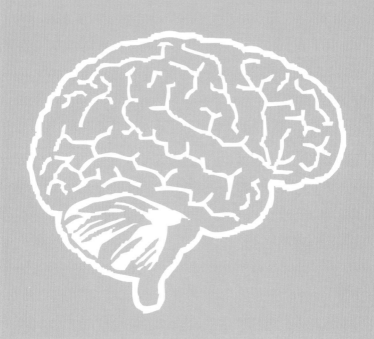

The complexity of the brain

The human brain is the most complex structure in the known universe. By means of it we are able to think, feel, and remember; to move our muscles and to maintain our balance; to fall asleep, dream, and then wake again. It controls our heart-rate, our breathing, and our body temperature. It also allows us to see, hear, smell, taste, and touch. As Hippocrates put it, "the brain, and the brain only, is responsible for, and is the seat of, all our joys and happiness, our pain and sadness; here is seated wisdom, understanding, and the knowledge of the difference between good and evil."

Facts and figures

- *The first recorded use of the word "brain" is found in the Edwin Smith surgical papyrus, which was written in roughly 1700 BCE.*
- *The heaviest documented human brain weighed 5 lbs (2,300 g).*
- *Albert Einstein's brain weighed only 2 lbs 11 oz (1,230 g).*
- *The average human brain measures 5½ inches (140 mm) (width) by 6½ ins (167mm) (length) by 3½ ins (93 mm) (height).*
- *The brain constitutes only 2 percent of total body weight; however, it utilizes 20 percent of the oxygen available to the body.*
- *There is no agreement about how many neurons (nerve cells) there are in the brain. However, the most common estimate is 100 billion, which allows for more connections between neurons than there are stars in the galaxy.*
- *Neurons are amongst the oldest cells in the body – in fact, we are born with nearly all the neurons that we will ever have.*
- *If all these neurons were lined up together, the resulting line would measure some 621 miles (1,000 km).*
- *The longest neuron in the human body runs from brain to big toe. It takes 0.03 seconds for signals originating in the big toe to reach the brain. In contrast, the smallest neurons are less than $\frac{1}{5000}$ of an inch in length.*

Brain size

Human beings do not have the largest brains in the animal kingdom. However, it does not follow that animals with larger brains – such as elephants and whales – are more intelligent than humans. There is no direct relationship between brain size and intelligence. In fact, brain size is correlated with animal size: the larger the animal, the larger the brain.

ABOVE The goldfish has one of the smallest brains in the animal kingdom, weighing just 1/333 oz (0.01 g)

Comparison of animal brain sizes

Animal	Brain weight	Animal	Brain weight
Sperm whale	17 lbs (7,800 g)	Tiger	9 oz (260 g)
Elephant	10 lbs (4,500g)	Lion	8 4/5 oz (250 g)
Human being	3 lbs 5 oz (1,500 g)	Sheep	6 oz (175 g)
Giraffe	1 lb 8 oz (660 g)	Cat	1 oz (30 g)
Horse	1 lb 3 oz (550 g)	Rabbit	2/5 oz (12 g)
Polar bear	1 lb 1 oz (500 g)	Guinea pig	1/7 oz (4 g)
Gorilla	1 lb 1 oz (500 g)	Hedgehog	1/10 oz (3.2 g)
Cow	1 lb (450 g)	Rat	1/14 oz (2 g)
Chimpanzee	14 oz (400 g)	Hamster	1/20 oz (1.5 g)
Orangutan	12 oz (350 g)	Goldfish	1/333 oz (0.01 g)

The nervous system

The brain lies at the heart of the nervous system – a highly complex system that variously: controls the automatic mechanisms of the body, processes sensory data, underpins decision making, allows us to move our muscles, and determines pain responses.

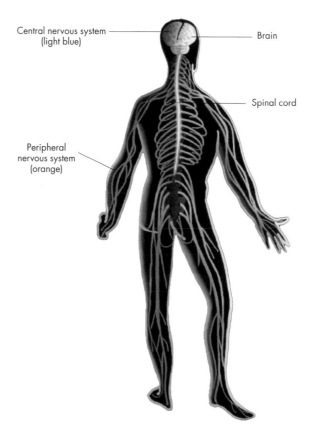

Central nervous system (light blue)

Brain

Spinal cord

Peripheral nervous system (orange)

ABOVE The human nervous system. The brain and spinal cord constitute the central nervous system (CNS). Nerves outside of the CNS are part of the peripheral nervous system.

The nervous system is made up of two different parts:

The Central Nervous System (CNS): *comprises the brain and the spinal cord, and it controls and regulates most of the functions of the body and mind.*

The Peripheral Nervous System (PNS): *resides outside the CNS, serving the body's limbs and organs. It consists primarily of nerve fibers – built out of neurons – stretched out to connect the spinal cord to the rest of the body.*

Neurons

There are more than 50 different kinds of neuron, each varying in size and weight. Nevertheless, neurons have a common structure.

A neuron consists of a cell body (the soma) with two arms (the dendrite and the axon) which enable it to communicate with the network of neurons that constitutes the brain. The tree-like dendrite receives signals from other neurons, whilst the axon passes a signal down its long, thin structure, so it can be transmitted to neighboring neurons. The brain is made up of 100 billion neurons, each one able to receive data from thousands of other neurons. It is this arrangement that underpins the vast complexity of the brain.

FACT
In July 2007, French doctors reported the unusual case of a civil servant who had no brain. Scans of the 44-year-old man's head showed that a huge fluid-filled chamber called a ventricle took up most of the room in his skull, leaving little more than a thin sheet of actual brain tissue. Intelligence tests showed the man had an IQ of 75, below the average score of 100 but not considered mentally retarded or disabled.

How do neurons talk to each other?

Neurons transmit data to one another using an electrochemical process. At rest, the inside of a neuron has a negative electrical charge compared to the outside; or, to put this another way, a resting potential of about -70mV (millivolts). In this state, no signal is sent down the axon. A signal is transmitted only when the threshold charge for an action potential has been met. This occurs as follows:

- *Information is received by the cell's dendrites.*
- *It is sent as positively charged ions down to the Axon Hillock, which connects the cell body to the axon.*
- *If the total charge reaches the critical threshold (about −50mV) the neuron will fire an action potential.*
- *This involves positive (sodium) ions rushing into the neuron, depolarizing it, thereby sending an electrical charge down the axon.*

Synapse

Neurons transmit electrical charges to one another through the synapse. It comprises a synaptic terminal at the base of the axon, a small gap (the synaptic cleft), and postsynaptic receptors at the start of the receiving cell.

The arrival of an action potential at the synaptic terminal causes the release of neurotransmitters into the synaptic cleft (via the action of small containers of neurotransmitters called vesicles which flood into the cell's membrane), which then act upon the receptors in the postsynaptic cell, potentially creating a new nerve impulse and starting the whole process again.

Neurotransmitters

Neurotransmitters are chemicals that function either to amplify or reduce the signals that pass between neurons. They work by binding onto receptor molecules that are located on the surface of the membrane of the postsynaptic cell. This has the effect of either increasing or decreasing the likelihood that the postsynaptic cell will fire an electrical impulse.

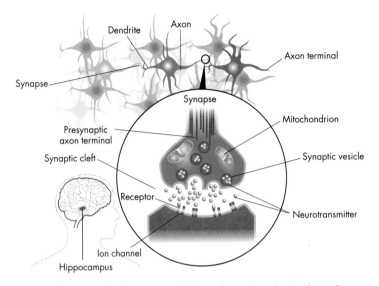

ABOVE The synapse is a key component of the nervous system allowing electrical charges to pass between neurons.

After a neurotransmitter has done its work, it is cleared away from the synaptic cleft. In the case of common neurotransmitters such as serotonin and dopamine, this occurs by means of what is called reuptake: the neurotransmitter is taken back into the presynaptic cell (this is why there is a class of antidepressant drugs called selective serotonin reuptake inhibitors which decrease the rate at which serotonin is taken back into the originating neuron).

Neurotransmitter systems

System	Major effects
Noradrenalin	Arousal
Dopamine	Cognition, movement, emotion
Serotonin	Emotion, body temperature, sleep, memory
Cholinergic	Learning, memory, arousal

Otto Loewi's dream

The German pharmacologist, Otto Loewi, was a light sleeper. In the middle of one night in 1921, he awoke with a great idea for an experiment, which he wrote down before promptly falling back to sleep again. The next morning, he found that he was unable to read his own handwriting. He then spent a desperate day trying unsuccessfully to recall what he was certain was an important idea. Happily he woke again the next night with the same idea, and this time rushed off to conduct the experiment immediately.

Vagusstoff

Loewi took two dissected frog hearts and placed them in separate containers surrounded by a saline solution. The first heart had its vagus nerve attached; the second one did not. Loewi stimulated the vagus nerve of the first heart with an electrical current, causing the heartbeat to slow. He then transferred some of the saline solution from the container with the first heart and applied it to the second one. After a short time, the second heart also slowed down. Loewi deduced that the stimulation of the vagus nerve had caused a chemical to be released into the saline solution which slowed the heart. He called this chemical "Vagusstoff"– it is now known as the neurotransmitter acetylcholine.

FACT

Research by Dr Olaf Blanke showed that if an electrical current is applied to the angular gyrus region of the brain then strange sensations can result. One female patient reported the experience of looking down at her own body from the ceiling; another had the feeling that somebody was standing behind her with malevolent intentions.

Regions of the brain

The way in which the brain tends to be divided up is enormously complex, partly as a consequence of the different interests that researchers bring to its study. However, it is possible to identify major regions and structures, and we now know quite a lot about what they do (although, of course, there is still an awful lot that we do not know).

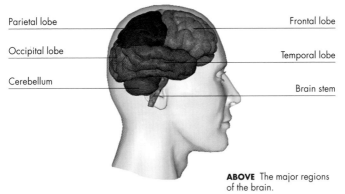

Parietal lobe

Occipital lobe

Cerebellum

Frontal lobe

Temporal lobe

Brain stem

ABOVE The major regions of the brain.

Maps of the brain

The Canadian neurosurgeon Wilder Penfield is famed for poking around inside the brains of conscious patients. This is possible because the brain has no pain receptors, which means that surgery can take place without general anesthetic. Penfield found that specific parts of the brain are associated with particular limbs and organs in the body. This enabled him to create "maps" of the brain – particularly the areas dealing with sensory and motor functions – which are still used today.

An interesting aspect of this work has to do with the temporal lobes (which lie at the side of the brain). Penfield found that when this area was stimulated, patients could experience vivid memories, or other experiences and hallucinations. Many of these experiences were quite strange, which has led some researchers to suggest that religious experiences might originate in this part of the brain.

Left and right hemispheres

The brain is split into two hemispheres, connected together by a bundle of nerve fibers known as the corpus callosum, which enclose most of the sub-cortical structures of the brain. The cerebral cortex, the famous gray matter of the brain, makes up the surface of the two hemispheres, and it is supported by underlying white matter (consisting primarily of long myelinated axons). Each hemisphere controls and receives information from the side of the body opposite to its location. Although it should not be overstated, there is evidence that the two hemispheres specialize in different kinds of tasks.

Brain lateralization

The expression "brain lateralization" is used to denote the fact that the two halves of the human brain tend to specialize in different tasks. This kind of specialization is seen most significantly with language, where more often than not it is the left hemisphere that deals with speech production and language comprehension. However, this is not true of everybody, with research indicating that up to 30 percent of people might have anomalous patterns of specialization. Generally speaking, the extent of brain lateralization tends to be exaggerated in popular culture – specialization exists, but it is not hard and fast.

Regions and functions of the brain

Major Regions	Sub-divisions	Structure
Forebrain	Telencephalon	Cerebral cortex; Basal Ganglia; Amygdala; Hippocampus
	Diencephalon	Thalamus; Hypothalamus; Epithalamus
Midbrain	Mesencephalon	Tectum; Tegmentum
Hindbrain	Metencephalon	Cerebellum; Pons
	Myelencephalon	Medulla Oblongata

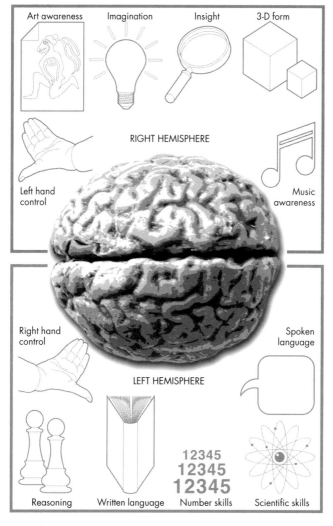

ABOVE There is some evidence to suggest that the left and right hemispheres specialize in different kinds of tasks.

Cerebral cortex

The cerebral cortex, the convoluted outer-layer of the brain, is the part most clearly associated with the higher functioning of human beings. It plays a central role in consciousness, attention, voluntary movement, memory, and language. Spread across the two hemispheres, it is divided into four lobes – frontal, parietal, occipital, and temporal – each of which is associated with a specific function.

The frontal lobe: *located behind the forehead, it is associated with higher functions such as reasoning, judgement, planning, language, movement, and memory.*

The parietal lobes: *found behind the frontal lobe, they are involved primarily in processing sensory information (visual and somatosensory, in particular) and in controlling spatial awareness.*

The occipital lobes: *located towards the back of the cortex, they deal mainly with vision, functioning to turn sensory data from the eyes into useful pictorial representations.*

The temporal lobes: *found at both sides of the cortex, they are involved in speech and hearing, and also in memory and emotion.*

The cerebral cortex, then, is the brain structure that is most clearly associated with those attributes that are distinctively human, particularly, the ability to reason, to use language, and to make plans.

FACT
The word cortex means "bark" in Latin, referring to the fact that it is the outer layer of the brain, varying in thickness from $\frac{1}{16}$ to $\frac{1}{4}$ of an inch. It accounts for about two-thirds of the mass of the brain and covers most of its structures. In higher mammals, the cortex is layered and folded. If the cortex from a human brain were laid flat, it would measure about 5 feet squared (1.5 m^2).

FACT

The basal ganglia, amygdala, and the hippocampus together form part of the brain's limbic system.

Basal ganglia

The basal ganglia system resides deep within the folds of the cortical hemispheres, and consists of three main structures – the striatum, the subthalamic nucleus, and the substantia nigra. It plays an essential role in the coordination of movement. The striatum is the main location through which other areas of the brain – particularly the cortex – connect to the basal ganglia system. A number of diseases are linked to the malfunctioning of the basal ganglia system. These include Parkinson's Disease, Cerebral Palsy, and Huntington's Disease, all of which involve disturbances in fine motor movement.

Amygdala

The amygdala, a small almond-shaped cluster of neurons located deep within the temporal lobes, plays an important role in regulating emotional responses, especially those associated with fear. Particularly significant is the part it plays in the formation and storage of memories of emotional events. Thus, monkeys without amygdalae find it difficult to associate a light signal with an electric shock, and also have problems associating a neutral stimulus with a food reward.

Hippocampus

The hippocampus, found in the temporal lobes, derives its name from its curved shape, which resembles a seahorse. Although its precise functions are not clearly understood, it is known to play a role in the formation, storage, and organization of memory. It is one of the earliest brain structures damaged by Alzheimer's disease, which has memory impairment amongst its first symptoms. It also seems to play a role in the storage of spatial information.

Thalamus

The thalamus – an egg-shaped structure found above the brainstem – plays an essential role in processing sensory information (auditory, somatosensory, and visual), and then transferring it to the cortex. It is not a simple conduit, rather it seems more akin to a communications center, which is able to filter data, relaying only that which warrants further conscious processing. There is also evidence that the thalamus functions to regulate arousal and awareness levels.

Hypothalamus

The hypothalamus is a small, highly complex, and tremendously important structure found just below the thalamus. It enjoys connections to just about every other part of the brain, playing a central role in the control and regulation of body temperature, sleep, desire, hunger, thirst, and the expression of emotion.

Brainstem

The brainstem is the lower part of the brain, stretching from the spinal cord at the base of the skull, into the middle of the brain roughly on a level with the eyes. There is an argument about precisely which structures it comprises. The most common view is that it includes the pons, medulla oblongata, and midbrain. It is the oldest part of the brain – indeed, it is sometimes known as the reptilian brain – and is involved in the control of heart rate and breathing, movement and digestion.

FACT
Locked-In Syndrome is a condition in which a person loses almost all ability to move the muscles used voluntarily, but retains their intellectual abilities. It is associated with damage to a specific region of the brainstem.

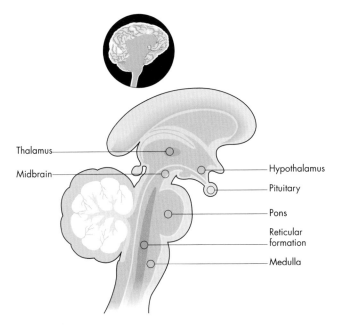

ABOVE The brainstem, sometimes known as the reptilian brain.

Tectum

The tectum, which is located in the dorsal region (near the top, towards the back) of the midbrain, consists of two parts: the inferior and the superior colliculi. These are involved in auditory and visual processing (including the control of eye movement), respectively. In birds and other lower animals, these structures are their auditory and visual systems.

Tegmentum

The tegmentum, which is found towards the bottom of the midbrain, comprises the red nucleus, substantia nigra, and ventral tegmental area. It is involved in controlling motor functions, and also in the regulation of awareness and attention.

Cerebellum

The cerebellum, found behind the brainstem, was one of the earliest structures of the brain to evolve. It has the appearance of a large walnut, comprising two hemispheres and a grooved cortex-like structure. It is important in controlling and regulating movement, balance, and posture.

- *Although it makes up only 10 percent of the total volume of the brain, it contains more than 50 percent of the brain's neurons.*
- *It is estimated that it is connected to the cortex by 40 million nerve fibers.*
- *The basic structure is shared by most animal species.*

Pons

Located on the brainstem, above the medulla oblongata, the pons is involved in relaying sensory- and movement-related information between the cortex and the cerebellum. It also has a role to play in the regulation of breathing, in the control of arousal, and possibly also in the activity of dreaming.

Medulla Oblongata

The medulla, which is located at the bottom of the brainstem (in effect, it is a continuation of the spinal cord), plays a central role in the control of autonomic functions (things over which there is no conscious control), including respiration, heart rate, blood pressure and digestion. It also functions to transmit nerve signals from the brain to the spinal cord.

THE BRAIN
THROUGH
THE AGES

Trepanation

Human beings have been fascinated by the brain for thousands of years. Indeed, there is evidence that the earliest systematically practiced surgery was a brain procedure called trepanation. This involves drilling a hole into the head to expose the outer part of the brain. We know from Neolithic burial sites that it was widely used in certain regions. For example, out of 120 skulls located at one ancient burial site, 40 had trepanation holes. It's clear that the practice was linked to religious and mystical beliefs – presumably the idea was that a hole in the skull would allow the evil spirit causing an affliction to escape.

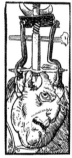

ABOVE Engraving depicting patients undergoing trepanation (1525).

Trepanation has been used to treat a wide range of diseases and disorders, including epilepsy, hydrocephalus, mental illness, and migraine. Rather amazingly, it is still used in the modern era, most commonly to reduce the pressure on the brain that occurs as a result of bleeding. Strangely enough, there are people who advocate trepanation for the healthy. The claim is that it increases blood-flow to the brain, thereby improving intelligence and creativity. However, there is no evidence to support this, and the procedure carries with it the risk of infection and blood clots. Nevertheless, the practice of trepanation remains notable in that it spans the entire duration of the interest of human beings in the brain.

The Ancients

The earliest recorded reference to the brain occurs in an Ancient Egyptian text, the Edwin Smith Papyrus, which dates from about 1700 BCE. The papyrus is a diagnostic and treatment manual that deals with injuries a soldier might suffer on the battlefield. It discusses 27 head injury cases, out of which about half show evidence of brain damage. Although the Egyptians had no understanding of how the brain worked, the papyrus nevertheless documents:

- *The convoluted appearance of the brain, which is described as being like "corrugated metal slag."*
- *The existence of a watery fluid that we now know as cerebrospinal fluid.*
- *The presence of the meninges – the membranes that protect the brain and the spinal cord.*
- *The fact that an injury can affect parts of the body a long way from the original problem (for example a paralysed arm or leg).*
- *Appropriate treatments for various injuries.*

An interesting facet of the papyrus is that it is relatively free of religious or spiritual thinking. The remedies suggested are mostly quite rational given the level of knowledge that the Egyptians were operating with (for example using a suture to close a wound).

It was originally thought that the papyrus was authored by Imhotep (widely credited as being the founder of Ancient Egyptian medicine), who lived during the Third Dynasty. However, the consensus now is that the text had multiple authors, and that it was put together over a time span of more than 100 years.

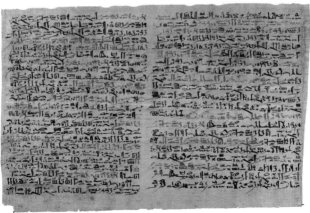

ABOVE The Edwin Smith papyrus is the world's oldest surviving surgical document.

Egyptian remedies and cures

The Edwin Smith Papyrus specifies three classes of injury: treatable, possibly treatable, and not treatable.

Not treatable: *"If thou examinest a man having a wound in his temple penetrating to the bone [and] perforating his temple bone . . . if thou puttest thy fingers on the mouth of that wound and he shudder exceedingly; if thou ask of him concerning his malady and he speak not to thee while copious tears fall from both his eyes . . . [this is] an ailment not to be treated."*

Treatable: *"His treatment is sitting, until he gains color, [and] until thou knowest he has reached the decisive point."*

Specific remedies: *Mix together the fats from a lion, a crocodile, a hippopotamus, an ibex, and a snake, then apply the mixture to the head.*

Apply an ostrich egg poultice to the wound (in this instance, on the forehead), then recant the following prayer (the only time the papyrus looks to divine intervention): "Repelled is the enemy that is in the wound! Cast out the [evil] that is in the blood, The adversary of Horus, [on every] side of the mouth of Isis. This temple does not fall down; There is no enemy of the vessel therein. I am under the protection of Isis; My rescue is the son of Osiris."

FACT

Alcmaeon's three-stage theory of knowledge holds that the brain is the source of the sensations of sight, hearing, and smell; that ideas and memory emerge from these sensations; that knowledge arises when ideas and memory become fixed.

The brain or the heart?

The Egyptians might have been aware that the brain played some role in the functioning of the human body, but they did not view it as being particularly significant. Rather, the common view was that the heart was the seat of wisdom and emotion. In fact, the brain was considered so insignificant that it was removed prior to mummification. In the words of Herodotus: "The most perfect process is as follows: as much as possible of the brain is extracted through the nostrils with an iron hook, and what the hook cannot reach is rinsed out with drugs." In contrast, the heart was never removed from the body: it remained necessary for the dead person to complete the journey into the afterlife.

Alcmaeon of Croton

It is generally accepted that the Greek physician and scientist Alcmaeon was the first person to identify the brain as the center of understanding. He also recognized that all the senses are connected to the brain. However, his ideas about how the senses work were very different from modern conceptions.

Vision: *occurs when things are reflected in the shining, translucent part of the eye (which is composed of fire and water).*

Taste: *the tongue is warm and moist, so consequently it is able to dissolve food, and thereby receive and transmit sensation to the brain.*

Hearing: *occurs when a noise is picked up by the outer ear, and then transmitted to an empty space in the inner ear, before being passed on to the brain.*

Smell: *passed along to the brain at the same time as breath.*

There is scholarly dispute about how Alcmaeon came to recognize that the senses are linked to the brain. The most likely explanation is that he had at some point cut out the eye of an animal, and observed that the optic nerve was connected to the brain.

Hippocrates

The ideas of Alcmaeon were developed by Hippocrates, who is generally considered to be the father of modern medicine. His greatness lies primarily in the fact that he pioneered an empirical approach to medicine; that is, he insisted that disease could be understood and cured by means of the careful observation and documentation of its nature. He also argued that all thought and sensation was controlled by the brain, a major departure from the then dominant view that the heart performed this role.

ABOVE Hippocrates, the "father of modern medicine."

The Sacred Disease

Hippocrates's naturalistic approach is perhaps best illustrated by the way that he sought to understand the condition epilepsy, which was known in Hipprocates's time as the Sacred Disease (because of its associated hallucinations, etc). He insisted:

- *It is no more sacred than any other disease, but rather has a natural cause.*
- *Those who first claimed a sacred cause were "conjurors, purificators, mountebanks, and charlatans."*
- *The brain is the cause of the disease, as it is of other great diseases.*
- *Specifically, epileptic seizures occur when the normal path taken by phlegm – the humor associated with the brain – becomes blocked.*

Of course, Hippocrates was entirely wrong about the causes of epilepsy – except to the extent that he put the brain at the center of the explanation – but his approach was radically new, and modern in the sense that it was naturalistic.

"Men ought to know that from nothing else but the brain come joys, delights, laughter and sports, and sorrows, griefs, despondency, and lamentations. And by this, in an especial manner, we acquire wisdom and knowledge, and see and hear, and know what are foul and what are fair, what are bad and what are good, what are sweet, and what unsavory... And by the same organ we become mad and delirious, and fears and terrors assail us, some by night, and some by day, and dreams and untimely wanderings, and cares that are not suitable, and ignorance of present circumstance. . . In these ways I am of the opinion that the brain exercises the greatest power in the man."

Hippocrates, ON THE SACRED DISEASE

Aristotle's errors

Not everybody agreed with Hippocrates that the brain was the body's control center. The most famous dissenter was the great Greek philosopher Aristotle. He argued that the brain could not be responsible for movement and sensation for the following reasons:

1. *The heart moves and contains blood. The brain is inert, incapable of sensation and without blood. Life is associated with movement, sensation and blood. Therefore the brain cannot be the control center.*
2. *There are simple organisms that move and have sensations, but which do not have a brain.*
3. *The heart is warm, the brain is cool. Warmth is associated with life, coolness with its absence.*
4. *It is possible to see the beating heart of an embryo before its brain is visible.*

The heart, therefore, is the "the Acropolis of the body."

Nevertheless, Aristotle did believe that the brain had a role to play in cooling the blood as it rose from the heart. So, for Aristotle, the brain was a kind of refrigerator!

Galen

The Greek physician Galen was the last of the great philosopher-scientists of the ancient world to make a significant contribution to our understanding of the brain. He is known primarily for his experimental techniques – in particular the dissections he performed on (non-human) animals (at this time religious sensibilities prohibited post-mortem experimentation on humans).

ABOVE Galen lecturing on anatomy in Rome, in the Temple of Peace, using animal skeletons. Galen's ideas would dominate western medicine for the next 1,500 years.

Galen shared Hippocrates's view that the brain was responsible for sensation and thought. He made perhaps his most celebrated discovery almost inadvertently when looking for the nerves that linked the lungs to the brain. Experimenting on a live pig, he cut a pair of nerves in its throat, which had the effect of silencing the pig though it carried on struggling. He deduced that he had found the "nerves of voice," which he then confirmed in a series of follow-up experiments on dogs, goats, and lions.

This finding that nerves from the brain – rather than from the heart, as Aristotle had believed – control the voice was confirmed in another set of experiments which showed that animals are able to carry on breathing and vocalizing if their hearts are exposed, whereas if pressure is applied to the brain they become silent and immobile.

Humorism

The four humors were believed to be bodily fluids that were essential to human health and happiness. The basic idea was that if they were in equilibrium then all was well. Illness was the result of blockages, overabundance, and so on.

The classical conception of the humors, associated with Greek physician Galen, has the following form:

Humor	Element	Organ	Personality
Blood	Air	Liver	Courageous, hopeful
Yellow Bile	Fire	Bladder	Angry
Black Bile	Earth	Spleen	Despondent, irritable
Phlegm	Water	Brain/lungs	Calm, unemotional

The theory of humors makes sense of treatments such as bloodletting, starving, and purging. The idea is that in these ways it is possible to rectify the harmful imbalances that cause disease.

Ventricles

The idea that the brain's ventricles – the hollow cavities in the brain – were the location of the rational soul came to prominence in the middle of the first millennium CE. The Christian philosopher, Nemesius, argued that perception was associated with the anterior ventricles, cognition with the middle ventricle, and memory with the posterior ventricle. Thus, for example, he claimed that if the anterior ventricle was damaged, vision would be affected, but intellect would remain intact. Unfortunately, this idea about the importance of the ventricles was completely wrong, and held up our understanding of the brain for hundreds of years.

The Moderns

For many centuries after the death of Galen, very little progress was made in our understanding of the brain (partly because of the dominance of religious orthodoxy). The Islamic Renaissance provided some advances in the documentation and understanding of neurological diseases and disorders such as schizophrenia, meningitis, dementia, and epilepsy, but it wasn't until the Renaissance in Europe in the sixteenth century that further advances started to be made.

Leonardo Da Vinci

The great polymath Leonardo Da Vinci was one of the first figures of the Renaissance era to take an interest in anatomy again. In an ingenious experiment, he injected hot wax into the ventricles of an ox's brain (the ventricles are a system of gaps in the brain that are filled with cerebrospinal fluid). He allowed it to harden, which provided a cast of the internal structure of the ventricles.

He was also notable for the accuracy of his anatomical drawings. The impact of his work was somewhat diminished by the fact that he was not prepared to challenge the orthodoxy of the time. This stated that the physiology of the body was properly understood in terms of the framework outlined by Galen (for example, Da Vinci thought that higher functions such as cognition and memory were located in specific brain cavities).

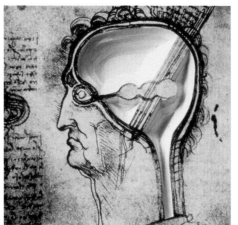

LEFT Artwork by Da Vinci of the head and brain chamber, an early diagram of the nervous system.

The birth of neurology

> "Among the various parts of the animated Body, which are subject
> to Anatomical disquisition, none is presumed to be easier or better
> known than the Brain, yet in the meantime, there is none less or
> more imperfectly understood."

Thomas Willis, THE ANATOMY OF THE BRAIN AND NERVES

Thomas Willis is considered by many to be the father of neurology.
His major work *Cerebri Anatome* was a dazzling tour around the
brain. For the first time, the main brain regions, cranial nerves, and
vasculature were specified and described with great precision.

Cerebri Anatome – the great leap forward

Breakthrough	Evidence
Established the importance of the cerebral hemispheres for higher functioning, particularly memory.	1. The human cortex is convoluted; the cortex of lower animals is not. Lower animals cannot learn and do not memorize in the same way as humans. The convolution is indicative of greater complexity. 2. Damage to the cerebral hemispheres can affect memory. 3. The cerebrum of two individuals with mental impairment was found during post-mortem to be unusually small.
Rejected the idea that the ventricles were the source of reason, memory, etc.	1. By exclusion – higher functioning was found to be associated with the cerebral hemispheres. 2. Observation – the ventricles are "vacuities."
Accurately described the corpus striatum for the first time, and established that it is important for voluntary movement.	1. Autopsies on patients who had suffered nerve disorders affecting movement showed impairment of the corpus striatum. 2. In newborn puppies movement is impaired; observation confirms the absence of a significantly sized corpus striatum.
Established many of the current terminological conventions for describing the brain.	1. He coined terms such as neurology, hemisphere, corpus striatum, lobe, etc. 2. One brain region – the "circle of Willis" – still bears his name.

Willis succeeded in establishing that specific brain regions are associated with specific mental faculties and functions of the body. However, he should not be considered thoroughly modern – for example, he believed that the cerebral cortex played an important role in generating and storing ethereal spirits.

Phrenology

Phrenology is the idea – first advanced (as cranioscopy) by Franz Joseph Gall towards the end of the eighteenth century – that there are specialized parts of the cerebral cortex associated with particular body functions, personality dispositions, and moral faculties. It suggested that it is possible to track these parts of the cortex by looking at the surface features of the skull. So, for example, a large bump on the skull would indicate an expansion of the cortex beneath it. It also suggested that it is possible to learn something about a person's character and behavior by tracing the pattern of bumps.

We now know, of course, that this is nonsense, but for a while it was an immensely popular idea – advocates and supporters of phrenology included such luminaries as Thomas Edison, Charlotte Bronte, Clara Barton, Ralph Waldo Emerson, Horace Mann, Herbert Spencer (though he later recanted), and Alfred Russel Wallace.

Although phrenology gained popular support, the scientific community was on the whole much more sceptical. By the middle of the nineteenth century, the discipline had been thoroughly discredited by the work of scientists such as Marie-Jean-Pierre Flourens and Paul Broca.

Rescuing localization

Although phrenology was shown to be a pseudoscience, the basic intuition that brain function is localized was correct. Evidence accumulated throughout the second part of the nineteenth century.

Marie-Jean-Pierre Flourens

Although Flourens was at the forefront of the campaign against phrenology, his research did lead him to conclude that brain function was localized in a broad way. He argued that evidence from brain regions indicated that higher functioning was located largely in the cerebral cortex, that the lower brain controls vital bodily functions such as respiration and circulation (thus Flourens noted that destruction of the brain stem resulted in death), and that the cerebellum played an important part in the management and integration of motor movements.

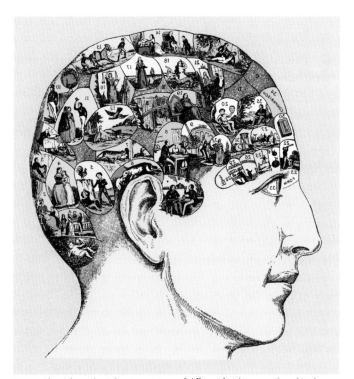

ABOVE Phrenology chart showing pictures of different faculties over the related area of the skull. For instance along the top of the head from left to right are depicted the characteristics of "benevolence," "veneration," and "firmness." (Published 1894.)

Jean Baptiste Bouillaud

Bouillaud argued that speech was localized to the anterior (front) lobes of the cerebral cortex.

He cited as evidence the fact that damage to these areas could leave intellect intact, but remove the ability to speak and vice-versa, that damage to other areas of the cortex did not necessarily affect vocal ability.

Simon Aubertin

Aubertin agreed with Bouillaud that speech was localized to the anterior cortex.

He cited the case of a man who had shot himself in the head, uncovering the brain. For a while, the man's speech and intellect were unaffected. However, it was found that pressure on the anterior lobes rendered him immediately mute, even if he was halfway through saying a word.

Gustav Fritsch and Edouard Hitzig

Fritsch and Hitzig conducted groundbreaking research that demonstrated that cortical localization extends beyond speech.

In a series of experiments in which they applied electrical charges to the exposed cortices of dogs, they showed evidence for the existence of a motor cortex that was further divided up into different areas corresponding to different parts of the body. For example, stimulating the cortex towards the front of the cerebrum caused the paw on the opposite side of the body to move. They also found that introducing lesions into the same area would cause movement disturbances.

Paul Broca

The French scientist, Paul Broca, was responsible for what was probably the definitive piece of research that convinced the scientific community that brain function is localized. Shortly before dying, a patient who went by the name "Tan" was referred to Broca. Tan suffered from a peculiar condition. Although perfectly capable of comprehending speech, he was only able to utter one word – "Tan" (hence his nickname). On the basis of the work of Bouillaud and Aubertin, Broca conjectured that Tan's condition would be caused by damage to the anterior cortex. This was confirmed by an autopsy after Tan's death, which showed an area of "chronic and progressive softening" near the temple of the left hemisphere, a region now known as Broca's area, and patients experiencing speech impairments caused by damage to this area are said to suffer from Broca's aphasia.

Broca's research was also significant in that it provided evidence for the "lateralization of brain function" – in other words, the idea that left and right hemisphere specialize in different kinds of task. The overwhelming majority of patients with speech deficiencies

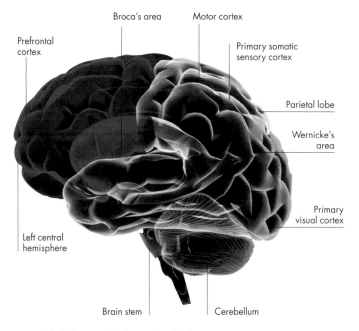

Broca's area　Motor cortex

Prefrontal cortex

Primary somatic sensory cortex

Parietal lobe

Wernicke's area

Primary visual cortex

Left central hemisphere

Brain stem　Cerebellum

ABOVE Each function of the brain is localized to certain areas.

examined by Broca had damage to their left hemisphere, which led him to the conclusion that it is the left hemisphere that is important for the production and understanding of speech.

Carl Wernicke

Wernicke discovered that damage to an area of the left temporal lobe close to the auditory cortex causes a disorder in which speech is fluent but meaningless. The damage associated with what is now known as Wernicke's aphasia is further back in the hemisphere than the damage linked to Broca's aphasia.

Wilder Penfield

As discussed in the first chapter, whilst operating on the brains of conscious patients, Wilder Penfield was able to determine that

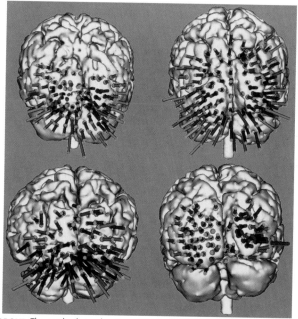

ABOVE The cerebral visual cortex, which controls vision. By knowing these areas, surgery such as tumor removal can be done with minimum damage to the visual cortex.

specific parts of the cortex are associated with particular limbs and organs in the body. This enabled him to create "maps" of the brain – particularly the areas dealing with sensory and motor functions – which are still used today.

Enter the neuron

In the middle of the nineteenth century very little was known about the cellular make up of the brain. The terms "neuron," "axon," "dendrite," and "synapse" were not yet part of the vocabulary, and scientists had no clear idea of how the nerve cells in the brain communicated with one another. After the structure of nerve cells became clearer in the 1860s, with the publication of the work of Otto Friedrich Karl Deiters, the most popular theory was that these cells were fused together, constituting a kind of nerve net.

There were two major factors impeding scientific research in this area: (a) existing microscopes were not powerful enough to observe matter at cellular level; (b) there were no adequate staining materials to isolate nerve cells from their surroundings. These problems began to be addressed towards the end of the nineteenth century, and then progress was rapid.

FACT
A person suffering from aphasia is unable to produce and/or understand spoken or written language. The disorder is caused by damage to those regions of the brain – almost always associated with the left hemisphere – that are specialized for language. An interesting facet of aphasia is that it is not restricted to verbal language which means that users of sign language will often lose their ability to sign if they become aphasic.

Progress of scientific research

Date	Progress
1860s	Joseph von Gerlach argues – incorrectly – that nerve impulses travel across a vast nerve net of interconnected fibers.
1886–7	Wilhelm His and August Forel independently suggest that nerve impulses might be transmitted without nerves being fused together.
1889	Santiago Ramón y Cajal made use of new staining techniques to demonstrate that the brain and nervous system is made up of discrete cells, work for which he received a Nobel prize.
1891	Wilhelm von Waldeyer introduced the term "neuron."
1897	Charles Sherrington hypothesizes the existence of a "synapse" as the junction between individual nerve cells.
1921	Otto Loewi discovers the first neurotransmitter – Vagusstoff (or acetylcholine, as it is now called).
1932	Sherrington and Edgar Douglas Adam win the Nobel Prize for their work on neurons.
1963	John Eccles, Andrew Huxley and Alan Lloyd Hodgkin win the Nobel Prize for their work on synapses in the peripheral nervous system.

Psychosurgery

Psychosurgery is brain surgery that aims at altering a patient's cognitive functioning. Although nowadays largely supplanted by less invasive techniques, it was a popular treatment for the severest forms of mental illness during the mid-twentieth century.

The first widely used form of psychosurgery was the prefrontal leucotomy, which involves cutting brain tissue in the frontal lobes by means of an instrument called a leucotome. Early results using the technique were encouraging – it seemed to improve the symptoms of patients who had previously been anxious, agitated or depressed. In the United States, the technique was popularized by the neurologist Walter Freeman – who subsequently developed a more radical form of the procedure, which came to be known as the "ice pick lobotomy" – and the neurosurgeon James W. Watts. By the early 1950s, more than 50,000 Americans had been lobotomized. However, doubts about the procedure were growing. There was little rigorous scientific evidence to support its effectiveness, and reports were accumulating of fatalities, infections, and patients being rendered inert and lifeless by the procedure. With the emergence of the first effective antipsychotic drugs, the technique quickly fell into disrepute, and is only very rarely practiced in the present day.

FACT

The New Zealand novelist Janet Frame narrowly avoided a lobotomy in 1951, after doctors were informed that she had won a national literary prize just as she was about to undergo the procedure.

Neuroimaging

One of the newest technologies that has emerged to help us understand the brain is neuroimaging (or brain imaging).

CAT: *Computed Axial Tomography builds a 3-D picture of the brain out of thousands of 2-D x-rays. The final image is produced using a computer algorithm.*

ABOVE Neurons are highly specialized for the processing and transmission of cellular signals.

PET: *Positron Emission Tomography similarly relies on computer algorithms to generate a cross-sectional image of the target organ or process. However, it differs from CAT in that it involves the introduction of a radioactive tracer into the body, which can be detected as it accumulates in the organ under examination.*

MRI: *Magnetic Resonance Imaging involves placing a subject within a magnetic coil, and then applying magnetic fields and radio waves in order to produce images of brain structures.*

fMRI: *Functional Magnetic Resonance Imaging makes it possible to see which areas of the brain are being heavily used at any particular time. Put simply, fMRI makes it possible to detect the presence of oxygenated blood in particular brain structures, which in turn makes it possible to see which parts of the brain are involved in accomplishing particular tasks, for example playing chess or solving a puzzle.*

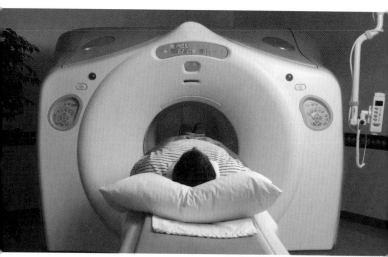

LEFT An MRI scanner builds up images of the inside of the human body.

EVOLUTION
AND
DEVELOPMENT

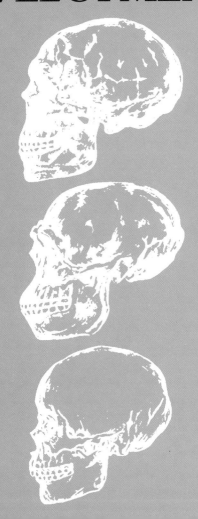

Evolution of the brain

Although there is a lot that we don't know about how the brain evolved, we do know that over the last 600 million years there have been four main changes in the way that nervous systems are organized.

1. *Brains have become more centralized and increasingly arranged according to hierarchical principles; specifically, they have evolved from loose collections of neurons — such as found in the "nerve net" of a jellyfish or hydra — to the complex, differentiated brains of the higher mammals that we see today.*
2. *Neurons and sense organs have increasingly become located at just one end of the body (a process called encephalization).*
3. *The complexity of the brain has increased — brains are now characterized by more and larger elements.*
4. *There has been a general development in the plasticity of the brain — that is the ability of the brain to respond to the demands of the environment, to store and retrieve memories, and to learn and exhibit novel motor skills.*

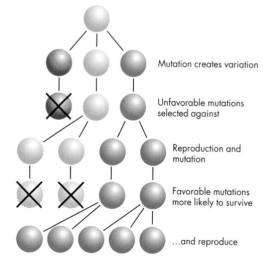

Mutation creates variation

Unfavorable mutations selected against

Reproduction and mutation

Favorable mutations more likely to survive

...and reproduce

RIGHT Darwin's theory of natural selection; favorable mutations within a species survive while the less favorable ones die out, allowing the species to evolve.

Natural selection

In order to understand how the brain could have evolved, it is necessary to know a little bit about how Darwinian evolution works. His theory of natural selection has the following basic form:

1. *The natural world is necessarily thoroughly competitive since any species will tend to produce more individuals than can be sustained.*
2. *Every species manifests some variation in the inherited traits of its members. So, for example, some foxes will be able to run faster than other foxes; some will have better eyesight, better hearing, sharper teeth, better camouflage, and better brains.*
3. *Variations that give an organism a competitive advantage (for example, a brain that enables an animal to plan a hunting strategy) will tend to be passed on more often than variations that put an individual at a disadvantage (for example, a brain that compels an animal to shout a warning before launching an attack).*
4. *Therefore, given enough time, helpful variations will come to be much more numerous than less helpful variations.*
5. *So long as there are always new variations for natural selection to operate upon, then evolution will carry on in this way.*

FACT
Darwin is remembered by history as the originator of the theory of evolution by natural selection. However, what is not so well known is that the British naturalist, Alfred Russel Wallace, also independently came up with the idea. Darwin rightly gets the credit because he got there first, and because his ideas were backed up by twenty years of natural history research and a mass of observational data.

Invertebrates

The simplest nervous systems are not brains, as such, but rather networks of separate but interconnected nerve cells termed "nerve nets." The jellyfish is the most notable example of an organism with a nerve net. The application of a stimulus to the body of a jellyfish will cause a reaction in the nerve net that radiates outward in a kind of rippling effect.

Jellyfish have structures called rhopalia which are involved in light detection, chemical detection, touch, and balance. Their effect is to provide the jellyfish with the ability to react to food and danger; to determine whether it is moving up or down; and to know whether it is moving toward light or away from light.

Nerve nets are associated with the phylum called Cnidaria. Other organisms that have nerve nets include the hydra and the anemone.

The curious eyes of the box jellyfish

Although not a true jellyfish (the box jellyfish is part of the Cubozoa class; true jellyfish belong to the Scyphozoa class), the box jelly also makes use of a nerve net. However, unlike true jellyfish, box jellies have an active visual system comprising twenty-four eyes. These are distributed in separate clusters of six, one cluster on each of the four

FACT

It was only in the eighteenth century that jellyfish were first recognized to be animals. Up until then, they had been considered plants. This is perhaps not surprising, since they do not have specific respiratory, circulatory, digestive or central nervous systems (as we have already seen). However, this turns out not to be an impediment to a long life, since one species of jellyfish, *Turritopsis nutricula*, has achieved immortality by endlessly cycling between states of sexual maturity and immaturity.

sides of the box jelly's body. Sixteen of the eyes are simple light-sensitive pits; two eyes in each cluster are comparatively sophisticated, and are capable of producing sharp images. However they do not in fact do so, since the box jelly's retina is too close to the eye to be at the optimum point of focus. The image is blurred.

This is not the only curious thing about box jellies. They also have no brain, nor anything else that looks like it could process sensory information. In fact, at this current time, we do not know how the box jelly handles the visual information that arrives from its multiple eyes.

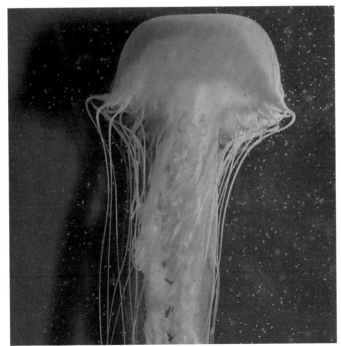

ABOVE Box jellyfish are best known for the extremely powerful venom. Stings from such species are excruciatingly painful, and are often fatal.

The worm

The worm has the least complicated central nervous system of any organism. The flatworm – the simplest of the worms – has two brain-like structures called ganglia at one end, and then cords running down the side of its body. It also has receptors connected to the ganglia that enable it to detect light and food.

The earthworm – the most common worm – has a very simple "brain" which is connected to a nerve cord that extends down the length of its body. This is the basic design for every organism that has a central nervous system (human beings included). However, the brain is not vital for an earthworm in the same way that it is for higher functioning organisms: if you cut out its brain, it is still able to move, mate and feed.

The insect brain

The insect nervous system is of an order of complexity above the nerve net of the jellyfish and the brain of the worm. Its design, however, remains simple. It comprises a dorsal brain, and then a series of paired, segmented ganglia (collections of neurons) that are connected together by a nerve cord that runs the length of the body.

The first pair (the protocerebrum) deal with vision (they are connected to the insect's compound eyes); the second pair (the deutocerebrum) process information coming in from the antennae; the third pair (the tritocerebrum) integrate sensory information and connect the brain to the rest of the insect's ganglia (via the ventral nerve cord). Also significant is the subesophageal ganglion, just beneath the brain, which controls the mouth and salivary glands.

BELOW The insect brain and ventral nerve cord.

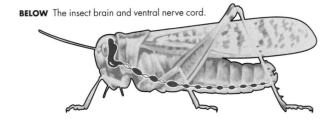

Although the insect brain is only a few millimeters in size, it is nevertheless quite capable. Not only does it process sensory information coming in from the antennae and eyes, it also enables insects to produce a wide range of behaviors, including:

Various forms of locomotion: *crawling, hopping, flying, burrowing, and swimming.*

Complex hunting strategies: *the female wasp will inject venom into a caterpillar in order to paralyze it, and then lay eggs on the inert body to ensure that her progeny will have a fresh supply of food when they hatch.*

Sophisticated navigational abilities: *bees do a complicated dance in order to let their hive mates know where food is located.*

The octopus brain

The octopus is generally considered to have the most sophisticated brain and nervous system of any invertebrate (an organism without a backbone). It consists of some 300 million neurons, many of which are found in the nerve cords of its eight arms. These are employed to help the octopus interact with its environment through suckers and chemical sensors, to move, navigate, and find food. The octopus is highly intelligent (comparatively speaking), manifesting both short- and long-term memory. There is evidence that it is capable of observational learning, though this is disputed. Octopuses can be trained to distinguish between patterns and shapes, engage in sophisticated hunting techniques (including seeking out lobster traps), and show impressive navigational abilities.

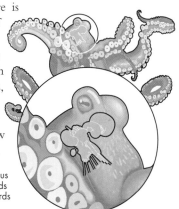

RIGHT Only part of an octopus's nervous system is localized in its brain. Two-thirds of its neurons are found in the nerve cords of its arms.

Enter the vertebrates

The first vertebrates show up in the fossil record about 500 million years ago, shortly after the period of rapid evolution that was the Cambrian explosion, though in fact they almost certainly evolved some time before this. The vertebrates include among their number the most highly evolved animals in the natural world, and this is reflected in the make-up of their nervous systems. The vertebrate brain consists of a series of structures which emerge out of a brainstem located at the top of the spinal column. The spinal cord, enclosed within the vertebrae of the backbone, transmits signals to and fro between the brain and the rest of the body.

FACT
Vertebrates belong to the phylum Chordata, which contains organisms that have some kind of supporting rod running down their back (a backbone in the case of the vertebrates).

The reptilian brain

In evolutionary terms, the oldest part of the human brain is the brainstem, which controls and regulates various basic functions such as heart rate and breathing. This is sometimes known as the reptilian brain, partly because of its evolutionary origins, and partly because it retains a similarity to the brains of modern reptiles.

The reptile brain has three main structures. The forebrain deals with abilities such as smell and taste; the midbrain with sight, and the hindbrain with balance and hearing. In early vertebrates, such as the amphibians, the forebrain was the largest structure because of the relative importance of the sense of smell. However, with the advent of terrestrial reptiles, the midbrain and hindbrain assumed more significance as auditory and visual data grew in importance. This explains in part the relative complexity of the reptile's brain compared to its vertebrate predecessors.

The triune brain

The triune brain is a model proposed by Paul D. MacLean that analyzes the structure of the human brain in terms of its purported evolutionary origins. The model proposes that the brain has three separate structures:

The cerebral cortex: *the rational brain, associated primarily with the primates (including humans), what MacLean calls "the mother of invention and father of abstract thought."*

The R-complex: *the oldest part of the brain, the brainstem and cerebellum.*

The limbic system: *comprising structures such as the amygdala, hypothalamus, and hippocampus (which came to prominence with the rise of the first mammals).*

The significant point is that this is not a top-down model where the cortex controls all the decisions over the other two structures. There will be occasions where emotions and desires associated with the more primitive R-complex and limbic system will take precedence.

Although MacLean's ideas have had a considerable impact on the public consciousness, they are by no means generally accepted within the scientific community.

FACT
Probably the first mammals to develop a recognizable cortex were the eucynodonts, which lived some 200 million years ago. They were excellent hunters, likely in part because their extra brain power enabled them to process sensory information from multiple channels, and also, in a rudimentary sense at least, to learn and plan.

Mammalian ascent

Whilst retaining the basic tripartite structure of the reptilian brain, the brain of the early mammals crucially added the cortex and the neocerebellum. The cortex is the great triumph of evolution, as not only is it the last part of the brain to have evolved, but it is also the locus of higher functions such as thought, memory, and learning.

In most mammals, the cortex is relatively small in comparison to the rest of the brain. But, it assumes a much greater importance in the brains of primates, and particularly human beings. In the human brain, the cortex is of such importance that it constitutes about two-thirds of the total weight. Just two and a half million years ago our close ancestors, the australopithecines – bipedal hominids – had a brain that was only about a third of the size of a modern human brain. So what happened? How did the human brain get so big?

The answer is that the cause of the rapid growth of the hominid brain over the last 2 million years is unknown. However, most explanations talk about two factors in particular:

The social hypothesis: *as our ancestors began to live in larger social groupings, so the opportunities for more sophisticated kinds of behavior arose. It is possible that this living style rewarded larger brains. Certainly we do know that there is a link between cortex size and the size of the social groupings within which animals live.*

Language acquisition: *language was likely a crucial step in the final stages of the evolution of the human brain. It opened up various possibilities, including:*

- *the development of shared ideas and skills*
- *collaborative planning rooted in conjectural reasoning*
- *a social structure based upon an articulated shared identity*
- *the emergence of a properly human culture.*

Big brains were likely favored by evolution because they brought rewards in terms of the development of shared skills, ideas, and culture that translated into longer survival, and therefore more offspring.

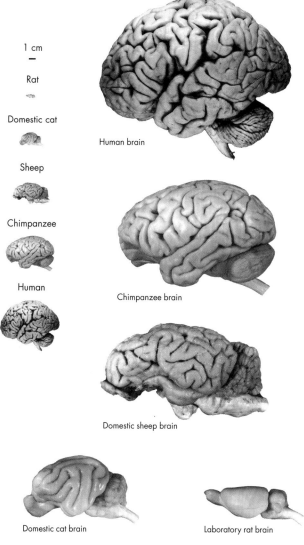

1 cm

Rat

Domestic cat

Sheep

Chimpanzee

Human

Human brain

Chimpanzee brain

Domestic sheep brain

Domestic cat brain

Laboratory rat brain

ABOVE Comparison of the brain sizes of various species of mammal.

Development of the human brain

Evolutionary change is not the only way of looking at the development of the brain. There is also a whole series of issues about its ontogenic development; that is, its development from a single fertilized ovum into the complex organ of maturity.

The basic story of the brain's development is as follows. About three weeks after conception, when the embryo is little more than a tiny disk, a neural tube emerges, which soon afterward develops three swellings that will become the forebrain, midbrain, and hindbrain. This process is driven by rapid cell division, specialization and migration. The major shapes of the brain are visible as early as the end of the first trimester, by which time it is also possible to detect electrical activity.

Two months later, the cerebrum is beginning to take on its convoluted appearance, and a simple EEG signal is present. Although the brain grows dramatically in size and complexity during pregnancy, its development does not end with birth. In fact, the brain is not fully mature until a person reaches puberty.

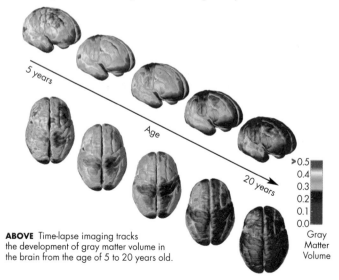

ABOVE Time-lapse imaging tracks the development of gray matter volume in the brain from the age of 5 to 20 years old.

Neuronal development

The early development of the brain sees the birth and controlled migration of billions of nerve cells. The process is remarkable, even if it is not fully understood. What we do know is:

- *Neural crest cells left over after the development of the neural tube migrate to many different locations in the body to help build the peripheral and autonomic nervous systems.*
- *The cell division that occurs in the wall of the neural tube in the early stages of development is staggeringly quick. A complete cycle of cell division to cell division can occur in little over an hour. It is this that underpins the geometric expansion of the number of nerve cells.*
- *Chemical signaling seems to determine whether the cells in the neural wall will become neurons or glia.*
- *Migration involves cells moving from inner parts of the neural wall to its outer edges. The bigger the neural wall becomes, the further the cells have to travel.*
- *This process of selective migration results in the neural wall thickening in such a way so as to begin to resemble the major divisions of the brain.*
- *The cerebral cortex develops from the inside to the outside; the deepest layers are constructed first, then the surface layers. This means that neurons have to migrate through existing structures.*
- *Specialized glial cells, adopting something akin to a "rope ladder" configuration, help to guide the migrating cells to their final destinations.*

To produce all the neurons in the brain, an average of 2.5 million new neurons have to be created for each minute of prenatal life. Once the nerve cells are in their correct position, a process of maturation and connection building begins. The axons of each neuron elongate in order to form thousands of connections with target neurons and muscles. This process is controlled at least in part by the way that a nerve cell's growth cone, located at the tip of its axon, responds to molecular cues. Broadly, if the cues are "attractive" then a connection is made, but if they are "repulsive" the growth cone will turn away from the signaling site.

Brain malformations

Brain malformations occur when the development of the brain is compromised during pregnancy, and almost always cause neurological deficits:

Agenesis of the corpus callosum: *associated with compromised vision, language difficulties, impaired motor coordination, and difficulties in swallowing.*

Lissencephaly: *causes impaired development, difficulties in swallowing, and a greatly reduced lifespan.*

Dandy Walker Syndrome: *associated with unsteadiness, lack of muscle coordination, or jerky movements of the eyes.*

Other malformations include septo-optic dysplasia, neuronal migration disorders, encephaloceles, and congenital hydrocephalus.

FACT
After two months the first sign of functional nerve activity can be elicited by stimulating the fetus, thereby provoking an avoidance reflex.

Anencephaly and Spina Bifida

Anencephaly and Spina Bifida are very different conditions. The former is a disorder in which a large part of part of the brain, skull and scalp are missing at birth. The latter is a disorder of the spinal cord that can result in disability. However, they both have in common that they are caused by the incomplete closure of the neural tube during the first five weeks of pregnancy.

The openings at either end of the neural tube are called neuropores: the anterior neuropore lies towards the front; the posterior neuropore toward the back. If the anterior neuropore fails to close the result is anencephaly; if the posterior neuropore fails to close the result is spina bifida.

There is no cure for anencephaly, and treatment is only palliative. The prognosis for anencephalic individuals is extremely poor. Normally the affected infant will be stillborn, and if not then only live a few hours or days. The prognosis for spina bifida varies according to its type, ranging from no discernible symptoms to lower-limb paralysis.

We do not yet know why the neural tube sometimes fails to close. There is evidence that there might be a hereditary component, and we do know that certain kinds of medication increase the chances of a neural tube defect. However, we are really only at the stage of saying that the causes will most likely be multiple, involving both genes and environment.

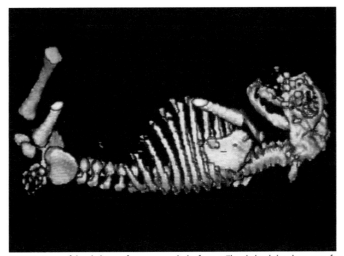

ABOVE Scan of the skeleton of an anencephalic foetus. The skeletal development of this foetus is well-advanced, except for the skull regions, particularly the cranium. Anencephaly results in incomplete development of the cerebral hemispheres of the brain, with fatal consequences.

Genes and environment

It might be tempting to think that the development of the brain is entirely determined by instructions laid down in the genes. This would be a mistake. The particular way that the brain wires itself up, and then modifies and tunes its synaptic connections and neural pathways, is fundamentally mediated by environmental factors. It is this that gives the brain its plasticity. At birth, the brain weighs 12 ounces (350 g), about a quarter of its final weight. A large part of the growth from infancy onward is accounted for by the expansion of the neuronal connections that underpin memory and learning.

Postnatal development

The brain does not stop developing with birth, indeed the synaptic connections in an infant's brain are neither completed nor fixed. The brain's plasticity lies largely in the ability of the cortex to transform and reorganize itself. This process occurs rapidly in the early years of a child's life before beginning to slow down. However, even if it is true that the numbers of neurons in the brain decline as we get older, it is a myth to think that the ability to develop new neuronal connections is inevitably lost with old age. Assuming that we do not

Brain growth

Age	Weight
Birth	The brain weighs some 12 oz (350 g)
6 months	About 50 percent of its final weight
1 year	Approximately 2 lbs (950 g)
2 years	75 percent of its full weight
5 years	90 percent of its full weight
10 years	95 percent of its full weight
12 years	Full weight approximately 3 lbs 5 oz (1,500 g)

succumb to a neurodegenerative disorder such as Alzheimer's or Parkinson's, we will retain this ability right into old age.

Neurodevelopmental disorders

The complexity of the mechanisms which drive the development of the brain means that there is a relatively large risk of developmental irregularities. In fact, numerous disorders have been linked to developmental problems, including:

Disorder	Effect
Attention Deficit Disorder	3–5 percent of school-age children
Language disorders	3–5 percent of school-age children
Learning disabilities	5 percent of school-age children
Epilepsy	1 percent of individuals
Pervasive Developmental Disorders	0.1 percent of individuals
Tourette Syndrome	0.5 per 1,000 individuals
Mental retardation	1 percent of individuals
Cerebral Palsy	0.2 percent of school-age children

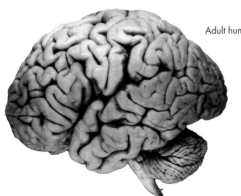

Adult human brain

Newborn human brain

ABOVE The average adult human brain (left) is 5½ ins (140 mm) wide, 6½ ins (167 mm) long, and 3½ ins (93 mm) high. A newborn's brain (right) is just a quarter of that size.

Cognitive and moral development

Postnatal brain development, not surprisingly, affects our cognitive abilities. This has been studied by psychologists under the rubric of cognitive and moral development. The two most significant figures in these fields are Jean Piaget and Lawrence Kohlberg.

Cognitive development

Jean Piaget's basic claim is that humans possess a genetically determined timetable that governs the emergence of particular cognitive abilities. The way a five-year-old experiences and interacts with the world differs from the way that a twelve-year-old will do so, which in turn is different from the way that an adult will experience and interact with the world.

Piaget argued that there are four discrete stages of development:

Stage	Age	Characteristics
Sensorimotor	0–2 years	Object permanence – the awareness on the part of a child that the objects he or she interacts with have a separate and independent existence.
Preoperational	2–7 years	The child develops the ability to use and manipulate symbols and language. However, there is little ability to apply logical principles; and the facility to generalize beyond what is immediately given has not yet properly emerged.
Concrete Operational	7–11 years	This stage marks the beginnings of the child's ability to apply logical principles. Also, there is a developing awareness of other points of view. The child is less egocentric.
Formal Operational	11–15 years	This stage is characterized by the ability to engage in abstract reasoning. It was Piaget's view that nearly everybody will acquire this ability by the time they are 20.

Although Piaget stressed that cognitive development was rooted in the fundamental makeup of the brain, he believed that learned environmental factors still have a role to play. Specifically, he claimed that intellectual progress occurs when a child is unable to assimilate novel experiences within existing mental schemas, and has to modify them as a consequence. Although Piaget's ideas have been subject to fierce criticism, his work remains tremendously influential, particularly in the field of education

FACT
Human beings are not the only species capable of object permanence. Higher apes, for example, are able to use mental representations in order to track the movement of hidden objects (for example, food hidden beneath one amongst many containers, which are then shuffled). This might not seem particularly impressive, but in fact most animals – including dogs and cats – do not have this ability.

Moral development

The psychologist Lawrence Kohlberg developed an idea called the Heinz Dilemma in order to test moral reasoning. The idea is not to elicit a right or wrong answer – indeed there may be no right or wrong answer – but rather to see what kinds of reasons people offer for their responses.

The Heinz Dilemma

Heinz's wife is dying, and naturally enough he is distraught and desperate to save her life. There is a drug that might help her, but it is only available in a single store. Unfortunately, it is extremely expensive, much more than Heinz can afford. He tries to borrow the money, but only manages to get together about half the cost of the drug. He goes to the storekeeper, tells him that his wife is dying, and implores him to sell the drug for less, or at least to allow him to pay the balance at a later date. The storekeeper says "No," despite the fact that he would still make a large profit on the sale. Heinz is so desperate that in the end he breaks into the store to steal the drug.

Did Heinz do the right thing?

Kohlberg argued that scenarios like these show that moral development occurs in stages – at different stages of their intellectual development people give different reasons for their moral judgements. So a young child, for example, will give different reasons for the conclusions that they draw about Heinz's behavior than an adult.

Kohlberg identified three levels of moral development, each in turn comprising two stages. Although he linked moral development to cognitive development, he did not think that it occurs inevitably as a result of growing older; rather, it requires that individuals work on, think about, and discuss their processes of moral reasoning.

Kohlberg's stages of moral development

Stage	Age	Response
Pre-conventional	Child to adolescent	Stage 1: Right and wrong is determined by authority and the possibility of punishment. (For example, a young child might think that Heinz did wrong because stealing is something for which a person is punished.) Stage 2: Will an action bring reward?
Conventional	Adolescent to adult	Moral reasoning is closely tied to membership of a social group. Stage 1: A good action is one that will gain the approval of others. Stage 2: A good action is one that is lawful and dutiful.
Post-conventional	Only 20 percent of population	Abstract in nature. References ideas of universal rights, justice, human dignity, the sanctity of life.

BRAIN AND
COGNITION

Human intelligence

Darwinian evolution has certainly created many wonders in the natural world: one thinks, for example, of the athleticism of the cheetah or the intricacy of a spider's web. However, the crowning achievement of evolution is the cortex – that part of the brain that gives us abstract thought, logic, problem solving, language, learning and memory. After all, it is possible that we are the only beings in the universe with these capabilities.

Definitions of intelligence

Linda Gottfredson et al: *Very general mental capability that, among other things, involves the ability to reason, plan, solve problems, think abstractly, comprehend complex ideas, learn quickly and learn from experience. It is not merely book learning, a narrow academic skill, or test-taking smarts. Rather, it reflects a broader and deeper capability for comprehending our surroundings – "catching on," "making sense" of things, or "figuring out" what to do.*

David Weschler: *The aggregate, or global capacity to act purposefully, think rationally, and deal effectively with the environment – an aspect of the total personality, rather than an isolated entity.*

Lewis Terman: *The ability to carry on abstract thinking.*

Alfred Binet: *Judgement, otherwise called good sense, practical sense, initiative, the faculty of adapting one's self to circumstances.*

Cyril Burt: *Innate, general cognitive ability.*

Robert J. Sterberg: *There seem to be almost as many definitions of intelligence as there were experts asked to define it.*

High intelligence societies

The most famous organization for people with high intelligence is Mensa International – to join which you have to have an intelligence quotient (IQ) in the top 2 percent of the population. However, there are other more stringent organizations, the most exclusive of which is the Giga Society. In order to join this select group you need an IQ score of 196. There are currently six members.

Society Name	Percentage	Percentile	IQ
International High IQ Society	5 percent	95th percentile	126
Mensa International	2 percent	98th percentile	132
Intertel	1 percent	99th percentile	137
Poetic Genius Society	0.5 percent	99.5th percentile	141
Infinity International Society	0.37 percent	99.63rd percentile	143
Cerebrals Society	0.3 percent	99.7th percentile	144
Neurocubo	0.2 percent	99.8th percentile	146
CIVIQ Society	0.13 percent	99.87th percentile	148
International Society for Philosophical Enquiry	0.1 percent	99.9th percentile	149
Glia Society	0.09 percent	99.91th percentile	150
ISI-Society	0.07 percent	99.93th percentile	151
sinApsa Society	0.05 percent	99.95th percentile	153
Vertex	0.009 percent	99.991st percentile	160
Prometheus Society	0.003 percent	99.997th percentile	164
The Ultranet	0.001 percent	99.999th percentile	168
Mega Society	0.0001 percent	99.9999th percentile	179
OLYMPIQ Society	0.00003 percent	99.99997th percentile	180
Giga Society	0.0000001 percent	99.99997th percentile	196

Measuring intelligence

There is little agreement about precisely what intelligence involves (though "abstract reasoning ability" is sufficient as a working definition). Consequently, many different kinds of tests have been proposed as a means of measuring it. These include: the Binet-Simon Intelligence Scale (1905); the Stanford-Binet IQ test (1916); the Weschler Adult Intelligence Scale III (1955); and the Cattell Culture Fair III (1957).

Intelligence testing normally requires that subjects respond, under a time constraint, to a series of short questions. The questions are designed to tap into what are seen as the various different aspects of intelligence. For example, the Weschler Adult Intelligence Scale (WAIS-III) includes items dealing with:

Vocabulary: *How well a person is able to comprehend and use his or her culture's vocabulary.*

Information: *How much knowledge a person has managed to acquire (for example, who was the first man on the moon?).*

Similarities: *The logic of similarities (for example, the odd one out between pear, apple and bicycle).*

Matrix reasoning: *Tracking the changes in a pattern across a matrix to determine what comes next.*

Arithmetic: *Mental calculation.*

FACT
Christopher Michael Langan is perhaps the cleverest man in the world. The one-time nightclub bouncer started talking at six months old, reading at three years old, achieved a perfect SAT score, and has a measured IQ of 195.

The sorts of questions asked under these categories will be familiar to most people who have completed an intelligence test. For example:

1. This is what is known as a matrix test. The idea here is to work out which shape is missing from the bottom right corner of what should be series of nine shapes.

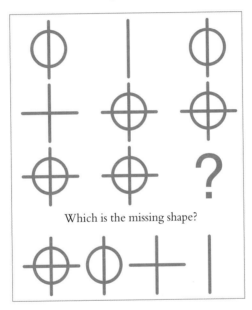

Which is the missing shape?

2. If it takes 40 people one hour to paint the Eiffel Tower, how long will it take 50 people?
   a) 30 minutes   **b)** 36 minutes   c) 48 minutes
   d) 56 minutes   **e)** 60 minutes   f) 66 minutes.

3. Paris is to Priam as Achilles is to …?
   a) New York   **b)** Bangkok   c) London
   d) Peleus   **e)** Ottawa   f) Sao Paulo.

(Answers at the end of the book.)

Intelligence Quotient

It is well known that modern tests of intelligence calculate something called an Intelligence Quotient (IQ). However, exactly what this means is less well-known.

The idea of something like an IQ was first mooted early in the twentieth century. At first, the idea was expressed simply as "mental age," any person who scored as well as an average 14-year-old on an intelligence test, for example, would be said to have a mental age of 14. The term Intelligence Quotient was introduced when this basic formula was developed to include a comparison with a person's actual age. For example, a 10-year-old child who scored as well as an average 12-year-old would have been said to have had an IQ of 120 – that is, 12 (their mental age) divided by 10 (their actual age) multiplied by 100 (to get rid of the decimal point).

However, there were difficulties with this formula – mainly that it doesn't work so well for adults – which led to it being replaced by a scoring system based on what is called the normal distribution (or Gaussian distribution).

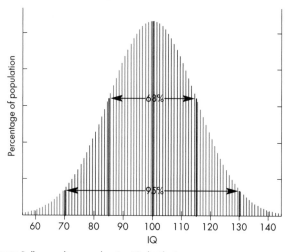

ABOVE Bell curve diagram showing IQ distribution.

This diagram tells us pretty much everything it is necessary to know about how IQ is calculated:

- *An IQ score is in essence a statement of rank. So, for example, a score of 100 is precisely in the middle of the distribution (it's the median) – 50 percent of people score less than 100, and 50 percent of people score more (not counting those who score exactly 100!).*
- *IQ tests are standardized on the basis of the normal distribution. This just means that a representative sample of a population will have piloted the questions making it possible: (a) to determine average scores (mean and median); (b) to ensure that different subsets of the questions will elicit identical distributions of scores (in other words, the test must be reliable – if you take it more than once, you want to be attaining the same score); (c) to ensure that this distribution is normal.*
- *Most people will tend to score around the midpoint (to express this more accurately, some 68 percent of people will score within one standard deviation of the midpoint). The further we get from average intelligence the fewer people we're likely to find. There aren't that many geniuses floating around.*

What do IQ tests measure?

This is where things get a little controversial. The evidence that IQ tests measure something is strong. In particular:

- *IQ tests are impressively reliable – repeat scores are highly correlated; and a comparison between different IQ tests also elicits a high level of correlation (for example, a person who scores 100 on WAIS-III will also tend to score around 100 on say the Stanford-Binet test).*
- *IQ tests have good face validity: that is, they seem to measure what they claim to measure. The main evidence for this is that people with high IQs tend to do relatively well in the kinds of pursuits where intelligence is likely to be a valuable asset (for example, education and employment).*

So if IQ tests do measure something, what is it?

There is an idea that there is no such thing as general intelligence; that in fact what we have are a range of different intelligences – for example, verbal, spatial, and mathematical intelligence. However, the evidence for this proposition is not strong.

The g factor

Psychologist Charles Spearman, with a statistical technique called factor analysis, established that across a whole range of intellectual tasks we tend to find that people who are good at one kind of task (for example, verbal reasoning) are good at all the others. The significance of this finding is that it suggests that there is a general intelligence factor (g) – there is such a thing as being generally smart. He admitted to not knowing what was involved in this g factor, but speculated that it was something akin to mental energy.

The IQ test controversies

Intelligence testing has attracted a lot of criticism, unfortunately much of it is politically and ideologically motivated. Nevertheless, there are genuine issues of concern.

Group differences: *There is a lot of data to suggest that there are IQ differences between social classes, races and the sexes. Most people accept that at least some proportion of these differences is real. However, whether the explanation for this is genetic or environmental (for example, poverty, cultural bias) is a matter of huge controversy.*

Reification: *Some critics (for example Stephen Jay Gould) claim that the results of IQ tests are nothing more than an artefact of standardization and mathematics. The criticism is that it's a mistake to assume that because you can construct a test to produce a certain result that it is indicative of the reality of a single causal factor (in this case, intelligence).*

Bias: *It is argued that IQ tests are culturally biased. Many IQ tests rely on time constraint in order to determine speed of mental processing. However, it is claimed that not all cultures place the same emphasis on the importance of speed; consequently, some people will be systematically disadvantaged by IQ tests.*

Political: *There is an objection that we simply shouldn't be doing IQ tests, particularly, where it involves comparing broad social groups to each other.*

Evolutionary psychology

Evolutionary psychologists such as Leda Cosmides and John Tooby reject the idea that the mind is a general purpose machine, arguing that it comprises specialized modules, each designed by natural selection to solve a specific problem from our evolutionary past. One piece of evidence for this comes from what is called the Wason selection test. Originally developed as a test of logical reasoning, it has increasingly been used to analyze the structure of human reasoning mechanisms.

The test begins with subjects being presented with four cards: the first one has a square on the front, the second a circle, the third the color yellow, and the fourth the color red. They are then told that every card has a shape on one side and a color on the other, and they are asked which card(s) have to be turned over in order to determine the truth of the proposition that if a card shows a circle on one face, then its opposite face shows the color yellow?

We are incredibly bad at this task. Only about 10 percent of people get it right. However, if you add a cheating scenario into the mix then suddenly people get the test right. This time the first card has the words "Drinks beer," the second "Drinks cola," the third "23 years old," and the fourth "19 years old." Which card(s) is it necessary to turn over in order to determine the truth of the proposition that if a person drinks beer then they're over 21 years of age? Now it's easy. You need to check the person drinking beer and the 19 year old (in order to determine whether they're drinking beer). Cosmides and Tooby argue that we find the first task difficult because we haven't evolved to do this kind of abstract logic, and we find the second task much easier because we have evolved an innate and specific ability to detect cheaters.

The solution to the first test is you need to turn over the circle (in order to check that the color yellow is on the other side) and the color red (to check that there isn't a circle on the other side).

Intelligence and the brain

If we accept, along with most psychologists, that there is such a thing as general intelligence, and that it varies between individuals, then it immediately raises interesting questions about the brain. What is it about the brain that makes some people smarter than others?

Brain size

There is some evidence that brain size and intelligence are correlated.

- *Intelligent organisms tend to have larger brains compared to their body sizes. The ratio of brain weight to body weight is 1:50 for humans, compared to 1:180 for most other mammals and 1:5000 for fish.*

- *MRI studies, which measure brain size much more accurately than cranial examinations, show that size is moderately correlated with IQ.*

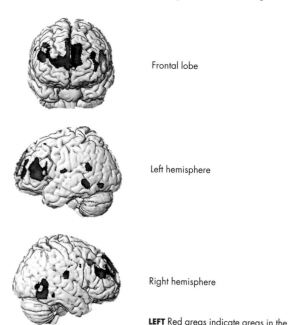

Frontal lobe

Left hemisphere

Right hemisphere

LEFT Red areas indicate areas in the brain activated by IQ testing.

Gray matter

As noted at the beginning of this chapter, the cortex, the location of the brain's gray matter, is the part of the brain most significantly associated with our intellect. Perhaps then high intelligence is related to larger volumes of gray matter. Certainly there is recent evidence to suggest that this might be the case. In particular, researchers at UC Irvine used MRI to measure the volume of gray matter in the brain of 47 normal adults who also took standardized IQ tests.

They found that the amount of gray matter in specific areas of the brain, rather than the overall size, was the key variable in explaining differences in intelligence. Moreover, it is possible that the fact that multiple brain areas are involved in intelligence explains why there is some variation in the ability of any particular individual to complete different kinds of tasks (for example, verbal, spatial, and numerical).

Genes or environment?

The vast majority of people accept that variation in intelligence is partly down to genes and partly down to the environment. Nevertheless, there is strong evidence that genes play the more important role. The key evidence comes from studies carried out on twins and adoptions:

- *The IQ scores of identical twins raised apart are more highly correlated than the IQs of non-identical twins raised together.*
- *Identical twins raised apart have IQs that are much more highly correlated than would be expected to occur by chance (that is, if the IQs of two random strangers were compared).*
- *The IQ scores of adopted children are more closely related to their biological mother than their adoptive mother.*

Memory

William James captured some of the mysteries of memory in 1890 when he asked: "why should this absolute god-given Faculty retain so much better the events of yesterday than those of last year, and, best of all, those of an hour ago? Why, again, in old age should its grasp of childhood's events seem firmest? Why should repeating an experience strengthen our recollection of it? Why should drugs, fevers, asphyxia, and excitement resuscitate things long since forgotten? . . . Evidently, then, the faculty does not exist absolutely, but works under conditions; and the quest of the conditions becomes the psychologist's most interesting task." (*Principles of Psychology*)

Three kinds of memory

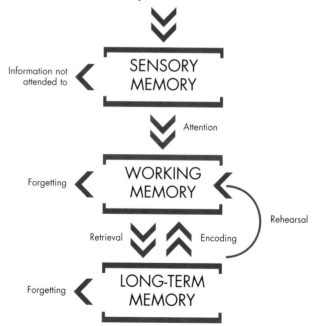

ABOVE Three types of memory.

Name	Duration	Capacity	Nature
Sensory memory	1 second or less	Large	Trace memory of incoming sensory data.
Working memory	10–30 seconds	5–9 chunks of data	The data we hold in our minds to accomplish our on-going daily tasks (remembering a phone number for the time it takes to dial it).
Long-term memory	A lifetime?	Limitless?	The store of (relatively) permanent memories – including memory of events and skills.

Sensory memory

Our senses are bombarded with information all the time. Before we are able to process this information it is held in a highly transient memory store. Part of what is interesting about sensory memory is that it seems to have a large capacity. However, the vast majority of the data we store in it is extinguished before we are able to pay attention to it (see George Sperling on page 74).

Working memory

The term "working memory" refers to our ability to manipulate information that is being held in a short-term memory store – as, for example, when we complete a multi-stage calculation in our head. Short-term memory is characterized by limited duration and capacity. However, there are techniques which allow duration and capacity to be extended.

Rehearsal: *The major technique whereby information can be held in short-term storage for more than 10 to 15 seconds. The best example of rehearsal – and the most cited! – is the repetition of a phone number in order to hold it in memory.*

Chunking: *The process by which multiple pieces of data are combined to form one piece of data. Consider, for example, the series: 2, 4, 6, 8, 10, 12, 14, 16, 18, 20. Although this comprises 10 pieces of data, it is in effect a single datum – even numbers up to twenty.*

Long-term memory

To transfer information from short-term memory to long-term memory requires that it is encoded so that it becomes meaningfully integrated into existing information structures. If memories are successfully stored and consolidated in long-term memory then potentially they will be present for the duration of a lifetime (though this is a matter of some contention). The capacity of long-term memory is large enough that it will never become an issue during the lifetime of a human being. However, this does not mean that it will always be possible to access memories that have been stored. Certainly we know that retrieval problems are responsible for at least some forgetting.

Iconic memory

In 1960, George Sperling was able to demonstrate that we remember significant amounts of data for tiny amounts of time. His experiment had the following form:

- *He flashed a grid of three lines of four letters at people for a duration of 50 milliseconds. On average, they were able to recall four of the twelve letters – a success rate of about 35 percent.*
- *He then repeated the experiment, but also presented a cue immediately after the matrix disappeared which told people whether they had to recall the top, middle, or bottom line of letters.*
- *Under this condition, recall improved to about 75 percent – people remembered about three of the four letters in the required line.*
- *This means that the whole matrix must have been available to memory for a very small amount of time (because there had been no way of knowing in advance which line would have to be recalled). The reason that people were only able to recall a small part of the matrix must be that the memory is extinguished before they could attend to it.*

This kind of very short-term, visual memory has been named iconic memory (a subset of sensory memory).

Brain and memory

It is almost certainly the case that memory is not located in any one part of the brain, but rather is constituted by networks of neuronal connections that are laid down throughout the brain. Synaptic plasticity – the ability of neurons to strengthen and weaken their connections with other neurons – is key here.

The basic idea is that memory and learning are dependent upon strengthened connections. This makes a kind of intuitive sense. It is easy to think, for example, that practicing the piano in order to become proficient at it is all about laying down relatively stable patterns of neuronal connections. The reason why it gets easier as you go along is that you don't have to start afresh with each practice session: the more you practice, the more neuronal connections you have already built.

Long-term potentiation

There is evidence that something like this occurs in the case of long-term memory. The key process involved seems to be what is called "long-term potentiation" (LTP), which refers to a long-term increase in synaptic strength. This was definitively established by Terje Lomo and Timothy Bliss in 1973 (though it had been first observed some seven years earlier). They found that applying a high frequency stimulus to a cluster of nerves in the hippocampus of an anesthetized rabbit would strengthen and prolong the response to any future single stimulus. In effect, a communication pathway, which it was found could last for many months, had been established between sets of neurons.

There are good reasons to suppose that LTP is the cellular correlate of learning and memory. Particularly, it can be brought about by a single event of synaptic activation and the changes it brings are maintained over a long period of time. However, we do not know enough yet to be anything like certain of the precise role that it plays (if indeed it plays a role at all).

Theories of forgetting

There are a number of different theories of forgetting.

Trace decay: *Holds that forgetting occurs when the neural traces that constitute a memory fade away over time.*

Interference: *Forgetting happens as memories interfere with each other; this can occur proactively (earlier memories can interfere with the encoding and retrieval of later memories) and retroactively (later memories interfere with the retrieval of earlier memories).*

Motivated forgetting: *Holds that forgetting can occur as a kind of defense-mechanism when remembering might in some way be painful.*

When memory goes wrong

We have noted that memory is not located in any particular part of the brain. However, there is evidence that specific regions of the brain are especially important for memory function. There is no contradiction here: memory function requires more than just the existence of memory traces – not least, there have to be mechanisms of storage and retrieval.

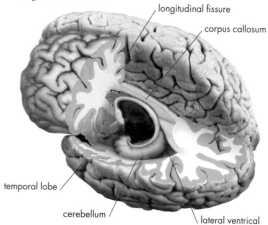

longitudinal fissure

corpus callosum

temporal lobe

cerebellum

lateral ventrical

ABOVE Illustration showing the hippocampus, situated within the ventral aspect of the cerebral hemisphere.

The case of Clive Wearing

Clive Wearing was a successful musician and conductor before he developed the illness – viral encephalitis – which destroyed his hippocampus, and damaged parts of his frontal lobe. He is now afflicted with one of the most severe cases of anterograde amnesia (the inability to form new memories) ever recorded. He experiences each moment as if he had just awoken from a long period of unconsciousness.

A constant presence in Wearing's life is Deborah, his wife. However, he experiences every meeting with her as if it were the first since before he became ill, which makes her visits emotionally charged. She only has to leave him for a few minutes, and he will greet her again with tears and whoops of joy.

The significance of Wearing's condition for neuropsychology is that it is a perfect demonstration of the vital role that the hippocampus plays in memory function.

The case of Henry M.

In his mind, Henry M. is stuck in the 1950s. He has no recollection of anything that has occurred in the last 50 years. The cause of his difficulties was an operation he had in 1953 which was designed to cure his epilepsy. Henry's surgeon removed his hippocampus without being aware of the effect that it would have on his memory. Over the last 50 years, neuroscientists and psychologists have learnt an awful lot about how memory works by studying Henry's case:

- *Short-term memory (including working memory) is different from long-term memory. It does not rely upon the hippocampus to form memories.*
- *The hippocampus is necessary for the storage of long-term memories. However, Henry M. is able to recall events from the time prior to his operation, which demonstrates that the hippocampus is not essential for the retrieval of memories.*
- *Henry is able to learn new skills. This shows that what is called "procedural memory" – the ability to learn new skills – relies on different mechanisms than "episodic memory" (long-term memory of events).*

Language

The ideas and research of scientists such as Jean Baptiste Bouillaud, Simon Aubertin, Gustav Fritsch, Edouard Hitzig, Paul Broca, and Carl Wernicke, established that verbal abilities – specifically, the production and comprehension of speech – are localized to the anterior and left temporal lobes of the brain.

However, there are also a number of interesting issues more generally concerning the brain and language, particularly those that surround the question of whether our ability to learn languages is in some way hardwired into the brain.

Noam Chomsky

Before Noam Chomsky came along, the dominant view about language acquisition was that it preceded in the same kind of way as other learning; namely, as a result of training and experience (in particular by the mechanism of selective reinforcement). The logic of this position is that there is nothing particular about the way the brain is wired up that makes it adept at picking up a language. Rather, it is just a function of the general plasticity that underpins learning and memory capacity.

Chomsky rejected this view. In his classic text, *Syntactic Structures*, published in 1957, he argued that human beings have an innate ability to understand the principles that underpin the structure of language. This explains how language users have the ability to articulate and understand a seemingly infinite range of sentences despite the fact that they will have only ever previously heard a tiny fraction of them. The details of Chomsky's theory are a little complex, but it is possible to get a sense of how it works:

- *The structure of language has two levels. Consider, for example, these two phrases: "The dog barked at the cat" and "The cat was barked at by the dog." These sentences have different surface structures (as is obvious from the fact that they look different!). However, at the level of their* deep *structure – the level of meaning – they are identical.*
- *Human beings are wired up to be able to move between these two levels*

of language. We are able to construct novel, but meaningful, sentences, because we are able to translate deep structure (the level of meaning) into surface structure (the level of particular utterances).

- *More precisely, Chomsky's idea is that people are able to utter meaningful sentences because they have access to a set of "transformational rules" that allows them to convert the meaning of what they want to say (that the dog decided to vocalize in the direction of the cat) into particular words and phrases ("The dog barked at the cat").*

- *The meaning of a sentence then is constituted by its deep structure; and the aptitude of humans for language resides in our ability to transform deep structure into surface structure – that is, meaning into words and phrases – by means of a set of innate, universal, abstract rules.*

The evidence for Chomsky's view is quite persuasive. The alternative view that language acquisition proceeds by means of the selective reinforcement of appropriate linguistic performance is unconvincing in the light of the fact that the number of sentences that children are ever exposed to is but a fraction of the number which they are able to generate.

But, perhaps more significantly the mechanism by which children are exposed to language – the spoken word – is an imperfect medium; people talk in incomplete sentences, they make errors, they slur their words, and in other ways corrupt the surface structure of their utterances. Yet children still learn language. And they do so easily, without much explicit guidance from existing language users. According to Chomsky, these, and other factors, can only be accounted for by the existence of an innate *Language Acquisition Device*.

FACT
The Italian cardinal, Giuseppe Caspar Mezzofanti (1774–1849), is believed to have spoken some 38 languages fluently, and another 30 or so less fluently. This makes him perhaps history's most impressive hyperpolyglot.

Non-human language

Non-human animals make use a huge variety of communicative gestures – both verbal and non-verbal – in order to transmit information. For example:

The bee dance: *Bees do a complicated dance to communicate navigational information to their hive mates.*

Vervet monkeys: *Employ a four-word alarm system to warn against different predators.*

Mimicry: *Songbirds, hummingbirds, and parrots all have the ability to mimic human speech, indeed parrots have been known to learn words and respond to requests.*

ABOVE Gold and blue macaws. Parrots do not have vocal cords, so sound is accomplished by expelling air across the mouth of the bifurcated trachea.

Cuttlefish: *Adopt special swimming postures along with gesticulations of their tentacles.*

Crickets: *Signal their presence by scratching the base of their wings, with each scratch a chirp is produced and together the chirps become a trill.*

Concave-eared torrent frogs: *Communicate via ultrasound and are the first non-mammalian species known to do so.*

Dogs: *Bark and whine, the barking being a throwback to the days of wild living and the whine being related to their desire for acceptance and wish to be looked after.*

Male mosquitoes: *Are drawn to the sound of the female's wing beat, a sound which is picked up on their antennae.*

Cotton-top tamarins: *Employ a wide vocal repertoire that is built out of combinations of two basic elements.*

Squid: *Communicate by flashing messages in colorful spots.*

Whale song: *Seems to be meaningfully involved in mating and feeding.*

Despite the rich communicative life of non-human animals, many scientists think that there are a number of features that distinguish human language from animal language. These include:

- *Human languages are almost infinitely plastic in terms of their communicative potential.*
- *Human language has two levels — surface and deep (semantic).*
- *In human language, there is normally no relationship between sound/sign and its meaning (the relation is arbitrary).*
- *Human language is employed with often subtle communicative intent (consider, for example, irony).*
- *Human language is constrained neither to the local nor the immediate (for example, it can reference both past and future).*
- *Humans are not restricted in terms of the languages they learn; nor the point at which they learn them (although there is a lot of evidence that it's easier to learn a language when you're young).*

The talking chimpanzee

It was thought possible that the reason that some animals – particularly primates – did not talk was because they lacked sufficiently sophisticated vocal apparatus. To test this theory, Allen and Beatrix Gardner adopted a 10-month-old chimp named Washoe, and attempted to teach her American Sign Language. It was claimed that the experiment was a success.

- *Washoe spontaneously employed the ASL sign for "More" in contexts where it had not been originally learnt, therefore – it was argued – showing that she had a sense of its meaning.*
- *She could reliably use about 250 different signs.*
- *According to Harvard psychologist Roger Brown, a report that Washoe had signed "water" and "bird" when she saw a swan was "like getting an S.O.S. from outer space."* (Source: *New York Times*)

However, it is likely that Washoe's grasp of language was fairly limited. The results were not replicated with further chimpanzees,

which has fostered a suspicion that Washoe had simply learned to respond to cues (which a lot of animals can accomplish). Chimpanzees might be able to learn a rigid and highly circumscribed version of human language, but the weight of evidence suggests that their brains are just not wired up in the right way to master it properly.

LEFT Chimpanzee species are the closest living relatives to humans.

BRAIN AND MIND

Mind and body

The concept of "mind" normally refers to any of the brain's conscious processes, and indeed it can be expanded to include unconscious processes. The previous chapter looked at the information processing aspects of the mind (intellect and memory, in particular). Here we look at some of its other aspects.

One of the great mysteries still be to solved is how it is possible to get mind (consciousness, thought, feeling, and so on) out of the

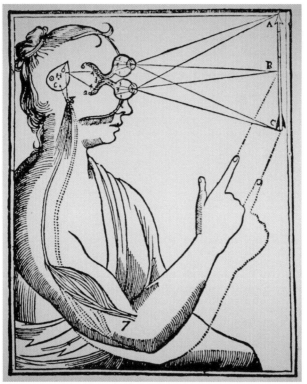

LEFT Illustration of the supposed relationship between the sensory perception of an image and muscular action, from a book by Rene Descartes *De Homine* (1662).

purely physical stuff of the brain. It is, to borrow a phrase from the philosopher Colin McGinn, the problem of explaining how it is that "meat" – that is, the brain – can think.

Philosophy of mind

Philosophical treatments of the relation between mind and body tend to fall into two broad camps: dualist and physicalist. Rene Descartes, perhaps the most famous advocate of dualism, argued that the mind was connected to the brain via the pineal gland – "the seat of the soul."

Dualism

Dualism holds that mind and body are in some sense different kinds of things. Exactly what this entails is complex (philosophers distinguish between substance dualism, property dualism, and predicate dualism). It is related to the intuition that there is a "felt" quality about the mind that constitutes its distinctiveness. Or, to put this another way, there is something that it is like to be conscious, whereas there isn't anything that it is like to be a chair or a pencil.

Dualists have different views about the relationship between mind and body:

Interactionism: *Holds that the mental affects the physical and vice-versa. If there is a "common-sense" view about mind and body this is it. We know that the physical world affects our experiences – try hitting yourself on the head with a mallet! – but we also think that the mind affects the physical world (for example, we can decide to move our arm). The problem for the interactionist view is that it is not at all clear how something non-physical (that is, the mind) can affect something physical.*

Epiphenomenalism: *The view that brain events cause mental events, but not the other way around.*

Parallelism: *The rather esoteric notion that mind and body do not interact with each other – only appear to do so.*

Physicalism

Physicalism is a type of monism, that is, it holds that only the physical is real, and that the mental (the mind) can be reduced to the physical (the brain). This is counterintuitive in that sensations — the "what it is like" character of pain, for example — seem not to be physical in nature (though they may have physical causes), but also plausible in the sense that the only stuff we know to exist is physical stuff.

Physicalists also have different views about the relationship between mind and body:

Identity theory: *The view that mental states are identical to brain states. Thus, to experience a desire for chocolate is no more than to have a certain arrangement of neurons in the brain.*

Functionalism: *Holds that mental states can be understood along the lines of a computational model — that is, in terms of their causal links with other mental states, and their relations to sensory inputs and behavioral outputs.*

Eliminative materialism: *The highly counterintuitive notion that there are no such things as sensations, perceptions and emotions — that these are simply misdescriptions that will be shown to belong to an outmoded folk psychology.*

> *"Tell me everything physical there is to tell about what is going on in a living brain, the kind of states, their functional role, their relation to what goes on at other times and in other brains, and so on and so forth, and be I as clever as can be in fitting it all together, you won't have told me about the hurtfulness of pains, the itchiness of itches, pangs of jealousy, or about the characteristic experience of tasting a lemon, smelling a rose, hearing a loud noise, or seeing the sky."*
>
> Frank Jackson, EPIPHENOMENAL QUALIA

Epiphenomenalism

Epiphenomenalism was first systematically espoused by Thomas Huxley at the end of the nineteenth century. It holds that mental events have no causal efficacy. Put simply, it's the view that the brain does all the important causal work, and that our consciousness, experiences, and sensations, are just along for the ride. A form of dualism, epiphenomenalism does not deny the existence of mental events, it just asserts that they do not do anything.

One of the major objections against epiphenomenalism is that it is highly counterintuitive. It just seems incredible to think that our mental life has no causal role to play in our behavior. It is rather troubling then to learn that there is at least some evidence coming from research on the brain that seems to support epiphenomenalism.

Readiness potential

The key evidence for epiphenomenalism comes from Benjamin Libet's experiments in the 1960s on readiness potential.

An RP is an electrical change in the brain that precedes a conscious human act – such as waggling a finger. Libet's discovery was that if volunteers are asked to waggle their finger within a 30-second time-frame, the RP that accompanies the waggling begins some 300 to 400 milliseconds before the human subject reports that they have become aware of their intention to waggle the finger. This is disturbing, because, as Libet puts it, the "initiation of the freely voluntary act appears to begin in the brain unconsciously, well before the person consciously knows he wants to act!"

However, it should be said that Libet himself does not believe that his research indicates epiphenomenalism, since the existence of a readiness potential does not commit a person to an action – there is still the opportunity to exercise a conscious veto.

FACT
Using cutting-edge brain imaging techniques, German researchers have been able to predict a person's decision some 10 seconds before they're aware they've made a choice, thereby casting doubt on the idea that we have free will.

Personality

It has been established that particular brain regions are associated with specific mental faculties; the Clive Wearing case showed that the hippocampus is fundamentally involved in encoding long-term memories. It is perhaps more difficult to believe, however, that something as nebulous as personality could be similarly localized. However, there is evidence to suggest that this is precisely the case, and even that specific regions of the brain are involved in the formation of personality.

Hans Eysenck's personality inventory

In a large dictionary, there are many thousands of words describing aspects of personality. The thought occurs then that perhaps a lot of these words belong together in clusters. For example, if we are told that a person is boisterous, bouncy, and bubbly, we might well conclude that these attributes are indicative of a more general personality disposition – and perhaps we'd label it extroversion. This is how psychologists tend to analyze personality. They attempt to show that there are broad personality factors which contain the more specific behavioral and personality traits that people manifest.

The British (German-born) psychologist Hans Eysenck was one of the first psychologists to use statistical techniques – specifically, factor analysis, the same statistical technique that led Charles Spearman to the discovery of the g – in an attempt to uncover these broad personality factors. It led him to identify two main dimensions of personality:

- *Neuroticism (Stable – Unstable)*
- *Extroversion (Extroversion – Introversion)*

Perhaps the most interesting aspect of Eysenck's approach is that he gave a thoroughly biological explanation, which referenced the physiology of the brain, for these different personality dimensions.

The key to the introversion–extroversion dimension is cortical arousal via the reticular activating system. The RAS stimulates the

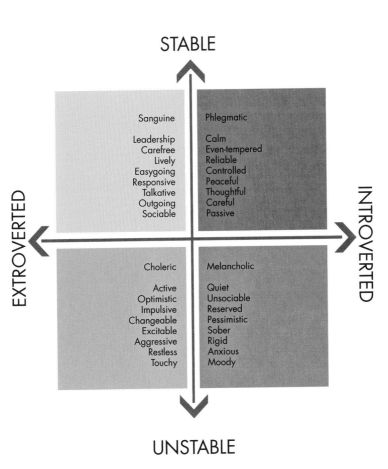

ABOVE Diagram illustrating the traits associated with each dimension of a personality. (A third factor, Psychoticism, was also added later.)

cerebral cortex, increasing arousal. The higher the arousal the less it is necessary to seek external sources of stimulation. The argument then is that introverts have naturally high levels of cortical arousal and extroverts naturally low levels.

A similar kind of analysis explains individual differences along the neuroticism dimension. Neurotic people show greater activity in the limbic system (primarily the hippocampus, amygdala, and hypothalamus), which is responsible for regulating emotional states such as aggression, fear, and sex. This renders them more susceptible to stress responses in the face of minor setbacks than emotionally stable people who have lower levels of activity in the limbic region.

> *"I always felt that a scientist owes the world only one thing, and that is the truth as he sees it. If the truth contradicts deeply held beliefs, that is too bad. Tact and diplomacy are fine in international relations, in politics, perhaps even in business; in science only one thing matters, and that is the facts."*
>
> Hans Eysenck, REBEL WITH A CAUSE

The Big Five

The "Big Five" is an alternative to Eysenck's model of personality which features five rather than three personality factors. These are:

Openness/intellect: *Imagination, curiosity, emotion, the desire for adventure, broad horizons.*

Conscientiousness: *Self-discipline, sense of duty, deferred gratification, goal-directed behavior.*

Extroversion: *Emotional expressiveness, excitability, sociability, energy, volubility.*

Agreeableness: *Cooperativeness, altruism, kindness, affection, trust.*

Neuroticism: *Emotionally unstable, anxious, irritable, sad, vulnerable.*

Sample test items (all items are Agree/Disagree)

Topic	Response
Openness/Intellect	I have a rich vocabulary.
	I have a vivid imagination.
	I have excellent ideas.
	I am quick to understand things.
	I use difficult words.
Conscientiousness	I pay attention to details.
	I always complete my chores immediately.
	I prefer order to chaos.
	I'm disciplined in my work.
	I always hit deadlines.
Extroversion	I am the life of the party.
	I'm happy to be around strangers.
	I make friends easily.
	I find it easy to strike up a conversation.
	I'm happiest when surrounded by other people.
Agreeableness	I empathize with other people's feelings.
	I'm on good terms with nearly everybody.
	I make people feel at ease.
	I'm soft-hearted.
	I make time for other people.
Neuroticism	I am often stressed.
	I worry about little things.
	I suffer from frequent mood swings.
	I get angry easily.
	I cry more than other people.

Cautionary note: If you answer "Agree" to all these questions, you're going to score highly on all these personality factors. If it were a real test, the questions would be mixed up so that responding "Disagree" would sometimes indicate the presence of the particular personality factor.

Brain injuries

Although the existence of relatively stable and distinct personality factors suggests that personality is rooted in the biology of the brain, there is other evidence that demonstrates this fact rather more dramatically. The story of Phineas Gage is exemplary in this respect.

Phineas Gage

Phineas Gage worked as a foreman on the railroads of America in the middle of the nineteenth century. One day in September 1848, he suffered a terrible injury when an explosion blasted a 13 pound (6 kg) iron rod right through his head. The rod penetrated his skull on the left side near his cheekbone, traveled upward past his left eye, and then exited the top of his head roughly at the midline.

Rather amazingly, Gage survived the accident, and though it was slow and difficult progress, he eventually made a near full recovery. But there was one profound and lasting effect of the injury – it completely changed his personality. He had previously been considered a model employee, but after the accident his employers would not give him his job back because he was too difficult.

We do not know exactly what caused Gage's personality change (indeed there is an argument that his personality changes have been exaggerated over the course of time). However, the most common suggestion is that it was a function of the destruction of parts of the frontal lobe that control emotion and decision-making.

"Elliot"

> *"Try to imagine it. Try to imagine not feeling pleasure when you contemplate a painting you love or hear a favorite piece of music. Try to imagine yourself forever robbed of that possibility and yet aware of the intellectual contents of the visual or musical stimulus, and also aware that once it did give you pleasure."*
>
> Antonio Damasio, DESCARTES' ERROR

"Elliot," a patient of neuroscientist Antonio Damasio, is a man without normal emotion. His problems started when he developed a brain tumor behind the eye sockets which grew to the size of a small orange, putting huge pressure on both frontal lobes of the brain and causing damage to the ventromedial prefrontal cortex. Successful surgery saved Elliot's life, left his intellect intact, but resulted in a radical change in personality.

Once a successful businessman, after surgery his life went downhill fast. He was unable to make even the simplest decisions. He would not dress himself in the morning, could not keep appointments, and was unable to complete routine tasks at his work. Consequently he lost his job and his marriage ended in divorce (indeed, he remarried and then got divorced again). In the end, he became dependent on welfare and the care of others to survive.

Tests showed Elliot to be intelligent, with properly functioning cognitive abilities, and a grasp of social conventions and moral values, but he was emotionally flat. When shown pictures of gruesome injuries and disasters, he displayed no physiological reactions (despite recognizing the emotional significance of what he was seeing). This affected his decision-making because he was deprived of the emotional cues used to identify reasonable choices from the multitude of possible choices. For example, we would never not get dressed in the morning because we instantly know the likely emotional consequences (embarrassment). Elliot did not have access to this kind of intuitive emotional data so in order to make decisions he had to work his way through an impossibly complex decision calculus.

FACT

At the age of 23, Rosemary Kennedy, the sister of JFK, underwent a lobotomy, in an effort to cure what her father complained were uncontrollable mood swings. It did indeed cure her moodiness. It also rendered her infantile, unintelligible, and incontinent. She lived out the rest of her life in an institution.

Problems associated with brain injury
Adapted from "Brain Functions and Map," Center for Neuro Skills

Affected area	Symptom
Frontal lobe	Paralysis
	Lack of focus
	Loss of spontaneity
	Mood swings
	Broad personality changes (as in the case of Phineas Gage)
	Broca's Aphasia
	Inability to solve problems
	Loss of ability to plan multi-layered tasks, such as making toast
Parietal lobe	Reading difficulties
	Problems with simple math calculations
	Problems with drawing objects
	Unable to name objects
	Inability to deal with more than one object at a time
	Inability to execute learned motor functions
	Loss of ability to find the words in order to write
	Inability to distinguish left from right
	Problems with hand/eye coordination
Occipital lobes	Illusions
	Inability to recognize words
	Absence of color recognition
	Problems with recognition of drawn objects
	Problems reading and writing
	Inability to locate objects in the environment
	Problems identifying movements of an object

Affected area	Symptom
Temporal lobes	Inability to recognize faces
	Wernicke's Aphasia
	Selective attention problems
	Short- and long-term memory difficulties
	Inability to identify and describe objects
	Changes in sexual behavior
	Increased aggression
	Non-stop talking
Brainstem	Breathing problems
	Difficulty swallowing
	Balance disturbances
	Problems with perception of environment
	Vertigo
	Sleep problems
Cerebellum	Problems with coordination of fine movement
	Tremors
	Dizziness
	Loss of rapid movement
	Inability to reach out and grab objects
	Slurred speech
	Loss of ability to walk

Disorders of mind and brain

The distinction between a disorder of the brain and a disorder of the mind is not clear. Some brain disorders, such as Motor Neuron Disease, have very little effect on the mind; others, such as schizophrenia, radically affect the mind; and a third group of disorders, such as psychopathic personality disorder, might not be associated with a distinct brain disorder at all.

Schizophrenia

> *"When people are acutely disturbed, they hear these voices as clear as a bell, as if it was someone talking to them. Indeed, often it will seem as if the voices are coming at them through a loudspeaker."*
>
> Professor Robin Murray, INSTITUTE OF PSYCHIATRY

The term "schizophrenia" roughly translates as "split mind." However, this etymology is somewhat misleading, since the illness has little in common with conditions such as multiple personality disorder (or, as it is now known, dissociative identity disorder). In fact, people with schizophrenia suffer a severely distorted perception of reality, which includes disordered thinking, delusions, and, above all, auditory and non-auditory hallucinations.

FACT

Five siblings – four sisters and one brother – of the Ulas family in southern Turkey are probably the only people in the world who routinely "walk" on all fours, in a kind of bear crawl. There is some dispute about what causes this behavior. However, the most likely explanation is that it is at least in part a consequence of a congenital disorder called cerebellar hypoplasia, which is characterized by the incomplete development of the cerebellum, a region of the brain associated with balance and movement.

There is no single diagnostic test for the condition. It is not possible to look at a person's brain under a microscope to determine whether they have schizophrenia. However, the illness does tend to present itself in a standard way.

Symptoms of schizophrenia

Symptom	Effects
Auditory hallucinations	Perhaps just a voice calling out a name.
Voices become more prevalent and systematized	They might shout abuse or bark instructions.
Delusions evolve to explain where the voices are coming from	For example, that aliens are in some way responsible for them.

It is important to be clear here that the voices are not in the head, as such – they are not part of an everyday interior monologue – but rather they appear to be coming from an outside source. The general pattern then is that people have bizarre hallucinations, they seek to explain them, which leads to delusions that function to reduce the anxiety associated with having such experiences.

Causes of schizophrenia

The predominant view about schizophrenia is that its symptoms – auditory hallucinations for example – are produced by a dysfunction of the brain. The dopamine hypothesis suggests that the problem is caused (at least in part) by an excess of dopamine transmission, particularly in the mesolimbic system of the brain. There is a lot of evidence to support this hypothesis:

- *All anti-psychotic drugs work by blocking dopamine.*
- *All drugs that increase dopamine can cause psychosis.*
- *Brain imaging shows that if individuals are given amphetamine, non-schizophrenics will produce only a small amount of dopamine as a result, whereas schizophrenics will produce a flood of dopamine – and the bigger the flood, then the more psychotic the individual.*

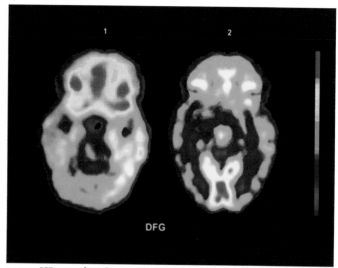

DFG

ABOVE PET scans of axial sections through a healthy brain (left) and a schizophrenic brain (right). The schizophrenic brain shows much lower activity in the frontal lobes.

The question of the origins of schizophrenia is more complicated. The orthodox view is that schizophrenia is a developmental condition – the brains of people with schizophrenia have developed in a slightly different way, which has made them more vulnerable to hallucinations and delusions. This might be the consequence of some brain trauma during pregnancy, for example. Anything which interferes with the development of the cortex will potentially disrupt neural systems, which in turn might render the brain less able to handle situations of stress.

There is also evidence that schizophrenia has a genetic component. Two genes in particular have been identified which seem to increase the risk of schizophrenia; a gene called neuregulin on chromosome 8, and another called dysbindin on chromosome 6. It would be wrong to suppose that the existence of specific genes – or indeed *in vitro* brain trauma – leaves an individual doomed to develop schizophrenia. In any particular case, schizophrenia emerges out of a complex grouping of genetic predisposition, environmental effect, and diagnostic process.

Treatment

With the development of antipsychotic drugs, our ability to treat schizophrenia has improved enormously. Gone are the days when schizophrenia wards were known as "snake pits." However, for about one-third of sufferers it is a disease from which there is little if any remission, and the severity of its symptoms means that it is associated with a high incidence of suicide. Although schizophrenics are often shunned and feared by the general public, the reality is that they are suffering from a disease which they do not choose, and over which they have little, if any, control.

Treatments for mind disorders

Talking Therapies

These come in many guises, including: counseling, cognitive-behavioral therapy, behavioral therapy, psychoanalysis, rational emotive behavior therapy, Rogerian psychotherapy, and neurolinguistic programming. The most successful of these is probably cognitive-behavioral therapy, which helps people to challenge the thinking processes that underlie their problems.

Drug Therapies

The treatment of mental illness was transformed in the mid-twentieth century with the emergence of antipsychotic drugs such as chlorpromazine and fluphenazine, which allowed many schizophrenics in particular to live near-normal lives. Conditions treatable by drugs include bipolar disorder, anxiety, insomnia, attention deficit hyperactivity disorder, and depression.

Electroconvulsive Therapy

A technique normally used to treat severe depression which involves using electric shocks to provoke seizures in patients. There is evidence of therapeutic effect in patients who have not responded to other therapies.

Other disorders of the mind

Unipolar Depression

Symptoms	Causes
Prolonged, unremitting sadness; diminished interest in activities previously found pleasurable; loss of appetite/weight; disrupted sleep patterns; restlessness; irritability; feelings of worthlessness; thoughts of death; inability to concentrate; reduced energy.	Genetic component; neurotransmitter involvement; women are twice as likely to be diagnosed as men; stress; a traumatic life event (for example, losing a partner).

Bipolar Disorder

Symptoms	Causes
Major depression (see above), plus episodes of mania, characterized by: euphoria, high energy, little sleep, self-confidence, creativity, extroversion, delusions.	Strong genetic component (stronger than in the case of unipolar depression); neurotransmitter involvement; right temporal lobe involvement.

Attention Deficit Hyperactivity Disorder (ADHD)

Symptoms	Causes
Poor concentration, impulsivity, short term memory problems, disorganization, inability to plan, poor discipline, disorganized ideas, tardiness.	Strong genetic component (though there is no single gene for ADHD); neurotransmitter involvement (particularly dopamine abnormalities); evidence that the frontal lobes, limbic system, and reticular activating system are all implicated in the disorder.

Autism

Symptoms	Causes
Difficulties interacting with others; communication problems; repetitive behavior; narrow interests.	Little is known about the causes of autism; strong genetic component; some evidence of the involvement of serotonin; no evidence of the involvement of the MMR vaccination.

Alzheimer's Disease

Symptoms	Causes
Cognitive deterioration (particularly memory loss, confusion, inability to learn, language breakdown); behavioral changes (agitation, mood swings, declining alertness, aimless behavior).	Progressive and widespread neuro-degeneration (the cortex, hippocampus and amygdala are amongst the brain regions particularly affected); genetic component; presence of plaques – clumps of the protein amyloid – in the brain.

Anorexia Nervosa

Symptoms	Causes
Refusal to maintain normal body weight; restricted food intake; obsessive exercise patterns; intense fear of gaining weight; preoccupation with food; distorted body image; denial of the dangers of low weight.	Genetic component; disturbed serotonin system; perfectionism.

Cotard's Delusion

Not all disorders of the mind are as well known as schizophrenia and bipolar disorder. Consider this report from 1788 of what later became known as Cotard's Delusion:

> *"An honorable old lady of almost 70 years sat fit and healthy in the kitchen and was preparing the meal as a draught coming through the kitchen door struck her so forcefully on the neck that she was suddenly completely paralyzed on one side as if hit by a stroke. She almost resembled a dead body during the following days. Four days later language returned and she demanded that the women should dress her in a shroud and place her in her coffin since she was in fact already dead. Every effort was made to dissuade her from this ridiculous delusion. Her daughter and servants made it clear to her that she was not dead but still alive. All was in vain, the "dead" woman became agitated and began to scold her friends vigorously for their negligence in not offering her this last service. Eventually everybody thought it was necessary to dress her like a corpse and to lay her out in order to calm her down. The old lady tried to make herself look as neat as possible, rearranging tucks and pins, inspecting the seam of her shroud, and was expressing dissatisfaction with the whiteness of the linen."*
>
> Charles Friedrich Pockels, GNOTHI SAUTON.

This is probably the first ever recorded case of Cotard's Delusion, which is the unshakeable conviction that one is dead. It has been encountered in schizophrenia patients, an MS patient, after brain trauma and during depressive episodes of bipolar disorder. Less than 100 genuine cases have been reported since it was first identified by Jules Cotard in 1880.

BRAIN AND
CONSCIOUSNESS

What is consciousness?

Consciousness is an imprecise term. It has been used variously to refer to awareness, self-awareness, the ability to experience pain and emotion, and sentience. Here it is used primarily to mean an awareness and responsiveness to one's immediate environment. That is not to say that we're only interested in consciousness when it is fully present, since distortions and absence of consciousness also tell us interesting things about the brain.

The question "What is it to be conscious?" might seem redundant, since in a sense we already know what it is like to be conscious. However, there are reasons why it is an important issue. For example, whether or not non-human animals are conscious is relevant in terms of the ethical issues surrounding their treatment; and whether or not machines are conscious will likely become an important question for similar kinds of reasons.

Characteristics of consciousness

There are a number of different ways in which an entity – which might include non-biological cognitive systems – may be considered to be conscious.

Sentience

This refers to the ability to be able to sense and respond to the world. However, what this entails exactly is much more complex than one might think. Consider, for example, that a computer-controlled robot can "sense" and "respond" to the world in quite a sophisticated way, yet we probably wouldn't want to take this as being indicative of consciousness (at least not at our current levels of

ABOVE Seventeenth century representation of consciousness.

technology). Similarly, it isn't clear that we'd be right to think that the nerve net of a jellyfish is sophisticated enough to produce consciousness, yet it does allow the jellyfish to interact with its environment in a rudimentary way.

Alertness

It is plausible that consciousness not only requires that an entity has the capacity for sentience, but that it is in fact alert and "geared into the world" (to borrow a phrase from the American philosopher Alfred Schutz). Obviously this criterion allows for degrees: we're all familiar with the experience of disorientation that occurs as we begin to fall asleep (during what is called the hypnagogic phase of sleep).

Intentionality

This refers to the directedness of consciousness – the fact that consciousness is always consciousness of something. Basically it is always directed towards an object: a person might perceive a cat, desire a chocolate, judge a competition, remember an anniversary, or contemplate a sunrise.

Self-consciousness

A more restrictive way of seeing consciousness holds that it involves some kind of self-awareness. In other words, for consciousness to exist it is not enough simply to be aware of some object of consciousness, it is also necessary to be aware that one is so aware. This conception of consciousness will almost certainly exclude many non-human animals, and quite possibly young humans as well.

FACT
According to Marvin Minsky, perhaps the world's leading cognitive scientist, humans have very little consciousness; that is, very little ability to know what's going on inside and outside ourselves.

The "what it is likeness" of consciousness

This is the subjective element of consciousness. William James expressed it like this: "Every thought is part of a personal consciousness . . . The universal fact is not 'feelings and thoughts exist,' but 'I think' and 'I feel.'" It finds its most famous modern expression in Thomas Nagel's insistence that "there is something that it is like to be a bat." Of course, this is nothing like what it is to be human, and we can't imagine what it is like, but nevertheless it is like something. More generally, Nagel argues that "an organism has conscious mental states if and only if there is something that it is to be that organism – something it is like for the organism."

Have modern humans always been conscious?

This sounds like a very strange question, but there is an argument that even in the relatively recent past humans were not conscious in the same way as we are today. In particular, in a book called *The Origin of Consciousness in the Breakdown of the Bicameral Mind*, the psychologist Julian Jaynes argues that human beings, even as recently as the time of the Trojan Wars, did not experience themselves as unified, conscious subjects. Part of the evidence for this proposition comes from an analysis of ancient texts such as *The Iliad*, and the older parts of the Old Testament. Jaynes notes that these do not make reference to internal mental states, and there is nothing in them to suggest that their writers had our kind of self-awareness.

FACT

Julian Jaynes has a radical interpretation of the role of the Gods in Greek mythology. He argues that people actually heard commands as if they came from outside their own heads, which they then attributed to the Gods, and this is reflected in early Greek mythology. He conjectures that these auditory hallucinations were related to the right brain equivalent of Wernicke's area and Broca's area.

Intelligent machines

"Not until a machine can write a sonnet or compose a concerto because of thoughts and emotions felt, and not by the chance fall of symbols, could we agree that machine equals brain…No mechanism could feel…pleasure at its successes, grief when its valves fuse, be warmed by flattery, be made miserable by its mistakes, be charmed by sex, be angry or depressed when it cannot get what it wants."

Geoffrey Jefferson, THE MIND OF THE MECHANICAL MAN

The question of conscious machines is becoming increasingly relevant. In February 2008, the renowned American inventor, Ray Kurzweil, claimed that "we will have both the hardware and the software to achieve human level artificial intelligence with the broad suppleness of human intelligence including our emotional intelligence by 2029." More dramatically, Stephen Hawking, Hugo de Garis, Bill Joy, Hans Moravec, Kevin Warwick and Martin Rees, all leading figures in their own fields, have argued that it is possible that human beings will one day be subservient to machines.

The Turing Test

But how can we know that a machine is conscious? The most famous approach to this question is the Turing test, named after the computer scientist, Alan Turing. In effect, Turing dodged the question of whether machines

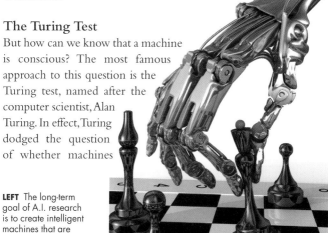

LEFT The long-term goal of A.I. research is to create intelligent machines that are able to reason and learn independently.

think (and more specifically have consciousness) by devising a test which would stand as a proxy for thinking (and consciousness). Its form is a variation on what's called "The Imitation Game." A man (Person A) and a woman (Person B) go into separate rooms. A third person (Person C) – an interrogator – then has a fixed amount of time to ask them questions in order to determine which of them is which. The role of the Person B is to help the interrogator come to the correct answer. Turing then asks:

> *"'What will happen when a machine takes the part of A in this game?' Will the interrogator decide wrongly as often when the game is played like this as he does when the game is played between a man and a woman? These questions replace our original, 'Can machines think?'"*
>
> Alan Turing, COMPUTING MACHINERY AND INTELLIGENCE

In essence, then, the test is simply whether a computer can pass itself off as a human during a conversation. If it can, then we can conclude that it thinks. Turing argued that this test can also be used as a substitute for the more specific question about consciousness since it would be possible to devise an interrogation that would aim to elicit the kinds of insights we tend to think are the province of conscious beings.

John Searle's "Chinese Room"

Perhaps the most famous objection to the Turing test as a device to detect the presence of thought is John Searle's "Chinese Room" thought experiment. Searle's objection is based on the fact that computers function by manipulating data based upon rigid sets of rules.

Searle imagines a situation where a person who knows no Chinese is locked in a room. In this room he is provided with a set of questions in Chinese, a batch of Chinese symbols, and a set of rules called "the program" that tells him how to manipulate Chinese symbols. In this way, he could provide answers in Chinese to questions in Chinese without having any idea what any of it means. But to the people on the outside it might well appear that the computer the Chinese room represents is able to understand Chinese perfectly; in other words, it might well pass the Turing test.

The objection then is that no matter how intelligent a machine appears, no matter how sophisticated the programming, it will never be intelligent, or conscious, because its internal states are purely syntactic (that is, rule-based); nothing semantic is going on.

The Loebner Prize

The Loebner Prize is an annual competition that celebrates the computer program best able to converse like a human being. The first winner in 1991 managed to convince 5 of 10 judges that it was a human being. Previous winners of the contest are:

Date	Winner	Computer program
1991	Joseph Weintraub	PC Therapist
1992	Joseph Weintraub	PC Therapist
1993	Joseph Weintraub	PC Therapist
1994	Thomas Whalen	TIPS
1995	Joseph Weintraub	PC Therapist
1996	Jason Hutchens	HeX
1997	David Levy	Converse
1998	Robby Garner	Albert One
1999	Robby Garner	Albert One
2000	Richard Wallace	A.L.I.C.E.
2001	Richard Wallace	A.L.I.C.E.
2002	Kevin Copple	Ella
2003	Juergen Pirner	Jabberwock
2004	Richard Wallace	A.L.I.C.E.
2005	Rollo Carpenter	George
2006	Rollo Carpenter	Joan
2007	Robert Medeksza	Ultra Hal

A.L.I.C.E. and Ultra Hal

A.L.I.C.E. (Artificial Linguistic Internet Computer Entity) is a "natural language processing chatterbot" – a computer program that tracks human speech patterns in order to produce its own conversational responses. Despite having won the Loebner prize three times and being one of strongest programs of its type, A.L.I.C.E. is unable to pass the Turing Test. Richard Wallace, the creator of A.L.I.C.E., is still working on the software that allows A.L.I.C.E. to mimic human conversation, and since 2001 various other programs have been able to make use of the Artificial Intelligence Markup Language used by A.L.I.C.E.

Ultra Hal – the 2007 winner of the Loebner Prize – is a chatterbot computer program that incorporates computer-generated characters within its interface, and which uses speech synthesis to create conversation. Like all chatterbot programs, it uses complex rules to create the illusion of intelligence whilst interacting with humans. Ultra Hal's practical applications include a "personal secretary" role, allowing it to remind users of appointments, dial phone numbers, and perform internet searches on demand.

ABOVE 2005 winner of the Loebner Prize, "George" can speak in 40 languages and with 2,000 people at the same time.

Animal consciousness

The first point to make about (non-human) animal consciousness is that in two of the senses we have identified it is obvious that animals have consciousness. They are able to sense and respond to the world, and they have a state of normal alertness. However, the much more interesting issue is whether animals have consciousness with a subjective feel and whether they are self-conscious.

Arguments against animal consciousness

Language: *Animals do not have language. Language is central to thought, and therefore consciousness. It follows that animals do not have consciousness. This line of argument was first articulated by the philosopher Rene Descartes. He argued that proper language is unbounded and creative, yet the best that any animal can do is to repeat words in a mechanical fashion. The fact that animals do not have language means that they do not have thoughts, since "the word is the sole sign and the only certain mark of the presence of thought hidden and wrapped up in the body."*

Behavior: *There is no behavior of animals that cannot be accounted for by unconscious processes. Kenan Malik, for example, points out that during the six million years since the evolutionary lines of humans and chimpanzees diverged, both species have evolved, but in a broad sense, give or take the capacity to crack open a few palm nuts or to hunt termites with a stick, the behavior and lifestyles of chimps are more or less the same as they were six million years ago. Yet this is clearly not the case with humans; moreover, it hasn't taken us six million years to get where we are – our lives have been transformed over the last 60,000 years.*

Self-consciousness: *Some evidence which suggests that only a few of the primate species have self-consciousness comes from mirror tests. Chimpanzees routinely interact with their own reflection if they see it in a mirror. About 40 years ago, the psychologist Gordon Gallup came up with an ingenious test to determine whether chimps are simply reacting to the sight of another chimp, or whether they recognize the reflection as their* *own. Having familiarized a group of chimps to a mirror, he anesthetized them. Half had a dye applied to their foreheads, half did not. After waking, on looking in the mirror, the marked animals were significantly more likely to touch themselves in the area of the mark, or in other ways respond to it, than the control group. Gallup's method has been repeated with many other species, but virtually none of them consistently pass the test (orang-utans are the major exception).*

Arguments in favor of animal consciousness

The ability to sense: *Some researchers argue that the subjective element of consciousness is identical with sentience. In other words, the ability to sense and respond to the world is coterminous with subjectivity, in which case most animals have subjective consciousness. This is the position of Michael Tye, for example, who argues that it applies even to honey bees.*

Language: *The Cartesian claim that animals do not have language has been challenged by animal language studies. Particularly, research showing that chimpanzees can communicate using American Sign Language suggests that their linguistic competence is greater than Descartes claimed. However, the language ability of chimps remains vastly impoverished in comparison to human beings.*

Behavior: *There are behavioral clues that suggest that animals have certain kinds of experiences in common with humans. In particular, their response to pain – vocalization, learned avoidance, fear, and the like – is*

FACT

Monkeys are happy to complete tasks for a reward. However, research by Sarah Brosnan and Frans de Waal indicates that if they see other monkeys getting a better reward for the same task – grapes rather than a cucumber, for example – then they will often refuse to complete any further tasks.

similar to a human response. Obviously this is not incontrovertible evidence that the experience is the same, but it is suggestive.

Anatomy: *The brain anatomy of all mammals is basically the same. Thus, if scientists want to learn about the human brain, they will often do their research on the brains of other mammals. This is the case with research into human pain. Its efficacy precisely depends upon the similarity of the mechanisms underlying the pain response. This lends at least prima facie support to the claim that mammals experience pain in the same kind of way as humans.*

Evolution: *A similar kind of argument can be made from the fact of evolutionary continuity. In other words, the fact that we share our evolutionary heritage with other mammals is at least suggestive that we might share the way we experience the world with them.*

There are no knockdown arguments in this debate. The fact that we cannot get inside the heads of animals means that we might never know for certain whether they have our kind of consciousness.

ABOVE Happy the elephant repeatedly touched a white cross marked on her head with her trunk which could only be seen in a mirror.

Different states of consciousness

Consciousness not only varies in nature and degree between species – and possibly between organic and non-organic entities – it also varies during the course of our daily lives.

Sleep

Sleep is a naturally occuring state of bodily rest and decreased responsiveness that occurs in all mammals and birds (and in many other species as well). It is conventionally divided into a number of different stages based on the characteristics of the associated brainwaves (as measured by EEG).

Stage	Effects
Stage 1	The lightest stage of sleep, observed at the onset of sleep or after waking in the night. It is associated with brain activity that produces theta-waves (4–7 Hz). Lasting from 10 to 15 minutes, stage 1 sleep is the transition period between wakefulness (which is characterized by what are called alpha-waves) and the deeper levels of sleep.
Stage 2	The point at which conscious awareness of the external environment switches off. Its onset is signified by the presence of short sequences (0.5–1.5 seconds) of waves called "sleep spindles" (12–14 Hz) and by big-amplitude wave forms called K-complexes (which last for about half a second and occur on and off throughout stage 2 sleep).
Stage 3	The first stage of really deep sleep, and it is characterized by large, rolling brainwaves called delta-waves (1–3 Hz).
Stage 4	Distinguished from the previous stage by a greater volume of delta-waves, this is the final stage of the four stages of what is known as non-REM sleep (NREM sleep). It is the part of sleep from which it is hardest to wake somebody.

The four stages of NREM sleep – which on average take about an hour to get through – account for some 80 percent of the total time that human beings spend asleep. As well as the brainwaves characteristic of each stage, NREM sleep is also associated with decreased autonomic nervous system function and (eventually) almost complete muscle relaxation.

After stage 4 sleep, the brain reverses back through the stages, and then after a brief period of stage 2 sleep enters a completely new phase of sleep called rapid eye movement (REM) or paradoxical sleep (so called because of the fact that its associated brainwaves are alpha and beta waves – the same waves that you see when people are awake). REM sleep has the following characteristics:

- *Rapid eye movements*
- *Alpha and beta brain waves*
- *Dreaming (or, more accurately, if you're woken from REM sleep then you're likely to remember any dream that you were having)*
- *Paralysis of muscles*
- *Penile erection in males; clitoral erection in females*
- *Raised heart-rate, blood pressure and metabolism*

Human adults will typically have four or five different episodes of REM sleep in a night, which adds up to about an hour and a half of time in that stage of sleep.

FACT
If you lose a night's sleep your ability to complete complex tasks will be severely compromised. If you lose three nights' sleep, then likely you'll be hallucinating. If a rat is deprived of sleep for twenty days, it will die.

Why do we sleep?

The answer is that nobody really knows. Various theories have been put forward, but they remain possible explanations rather than definitive explanations.

Memory consolidation: *There is a lot of evidence that sleep and memory are tied together in various ways. For example, if you deprive people of sleep then their working memory is significantly impaired.*

Evolutionary benefits: *There are various reasons why sleep might have had an evolutionary payoff. Perhaps the most persuasive explanation emphasizes the avoidance of danger. If you're a creature that is highly adapted to hunting under the cover of darkness, it's probably going to pay you not to be out and about during the day. Sleep is a fairly simple way of tipping the odds in favor of remaining hidden when you're supposed to be.*

ABOVE The Stuff that Dreams are Made Of, by John Anster Fitzgerald (c. 1858), one of a number of "dream paintings" by the artist.

Restoration: *There is evidence that sleep helps return the body to a state of optimal functioning. For example, studies show that an absence of sleep will result in a compromised immune system, an increased metabolic rate, and slower healing.*

Development: *There is some data that suggests that sleep might play an important role in early development. It seems likely that the fact that young children sleep a lot compared to adults is in some way linked to their development.*

Sigmund Freud on dreams

According to Sigmund Freud, dreams are a disguised expression of wish fulfilment. He comes to this conclusion as a consequence of an analysis that has the following form:

- *Human beings are subject to the demands of a libidinal energy – primarily sexual – which exerts a powerful and disturbing power.*
- *A reality principle exists which means that the libido cannot simply have free expression; it has to be repressed.*
- *There is also a domain of moral prohibition that is in constant tension with the desires of the libido.*
- *Denied physical expression, the libido will manifest itself through other means: sometimes perhaps neurotic symptoms; sometimes dreaming.*
- *Although the moral, censorious part of the mind is less vigilant during sleep, it still makes its presence felt.*
- *This means that any wish fulfilment in a dream has to be disguised; anything explicit would produce anxiety, waking the dreamer.*
- *Thus, dreams are disguised wish fulfilment. Their manifest content hides the deeper, hidden meaning of the dream.*
- *It is through "dream work," which is undertaken by a skilled – and expensive! – analysts that the latent meaning of the dream can be discovered and understood.*

Personality and the unconscious

A common idea, nowadays associated primarily with Sigmund Freud and Carl Jung, is that there are unconscious aspects of the personality that can drive behavior.

Freud

Freud's major thesis is that human behavior is driven by a dynamic unconscious over which we have little control: we often act for reasons far removed from our conscious intentions. This idea that personality has an unconscious aspect was not particularly novel. Freud's innovation was the claim that it is possible for a psychoanalyst to get at the contents of the unconscious by employing techniques such as word association and dream analysis. The hope was that by knowing the unconscious roots of our thoughts and behavior we would be in a better position to control them.

Freud was a practicing psychoanalyst. Many of his ideas arose directly out of his therapeutic experience. In one notable case study, he argued that the fear of horses experienced by Hans was in fact a manifestation of his fear of his father, which was rooted in an Oedipal desire for his mother, meaning his father was a kind of love rival.

By the 1920s, Freud had developed his tripartite theory of human personality, which holds that the human psyche comprises three parts: the id (a person's instincts), the ego (the rational, decision-making part of the personality), and the superego (the moral, censorious part). The id seeks the immediate satisfaction of

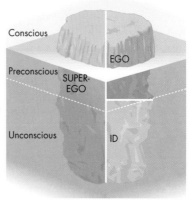

ABOVE In Freud's model, the reasoning, conscious mind is only a small part of the whole. The hidden, irrational id and superego lie outside of conscious control.

its desires; however, in line with a "reality principle," the ego has to balance the desires of the id against the demands of living in the world. It also has to keep the superego happy by ensuring that a person's behavior falls within the bounds of what is morally acceptable from the point of view of the superego.

It was Freud's view that many kinds of psychological distress are related to tensions between these aspects of personality. It is the analyst's job to bring these tensions to the surface, thereby reducing their power to harm.

Jung

According to Jung, the psyche is split into three interacting parts: consciousness, personal unconscious, and collective unconscious.

The conscious mind is the aspect of the psyche which is directly known to a person. Jung claimed that there are two personality types, and that most people will remain true to their personality type throughout their life. The "extrovert" directs libidinal energies outward toward the external world. The "introvert" looks inward, focusing on subjective feelings and experience.

Jung's treatment of the unconscious was unorthodox. He claimed that humans are wired up to experience and orient themselves toward the world as their ancestors did. These innate organizing principles of the collective unconscious are termed "archetypes." Examples include: the "persona" – the face we present to the world; "the shadow" – the source of our animal instincts; "the self" - the organizing principle by means of which we structure our personality; "the anima" – the feminine in the masculine; and "the animus" – the masculine in the feminine.

Unfortunately, there are big holes in Jung's theories. The idea that it is possible to inherit ancestral memories is ruled out by what we know about how inheritance works. It would require the inheritance of acquired characteristics (memories), which just isn't possible, at least not in any straightforward way (this is why if your father learnt to speak French as a boy, it doesn't follow that you can speak it too).

Altered consciousness

Perhaps the most common way that human beings alter their own consciousness is by the use of drugs.

Alcohol

Topic	Response
Action	Poorly understood. It seems to function by increasing the efficiency of GABA, an inhibitory neurotransmitter, which has the effect of dampening down neuronal activity.
Effect	Alcohol is a depressant. Hence its association with sleepiness, impaired motor movements, slurred speech, and so on. The euphoric feelings sometimes induced by alcohol come from the increased production of dopamine.

Caffeine

Topic	Response
Action	It functions by blocking the effect of the chemical adenosine, which normally dampens down neuronal activity. In the absence of adenosine, everything is shifted up a gear, which has the effect of pushing adrenaline into the bloodstream.
Effect	It increases alertness, heart rate, blood pressure, and respiration. Less welcome side-effects include sleeplessness, irritability, and anxiety.

Cannabis

Topic	Response
Action	The active ingredient, tetrahydrocannabinol (THC), binds to a receptor in the brain called cannabinoid receptor-1 (CB1). CB1 receptors are widespread throughout the brain, hence THC's system-wide effects. Exactly how CB1 produces its effects is not well understood.
Effect	Cannabis has a huge variety of effects, including: euphoria; altered perception; feelings of relaxation; hunger; lethargy; joviality; paranoia; pain relief.

Heroin

Topic	Response
Action	Heroin is an opiate. The brain has opiate receptors designed to bind onto endorphins, the body's natural painkiller. Heroin functions by binding onto these receptors, particularly in the region of the brain known as the corpus striatum.
Effect	Heroin produces intense euphoria, and acts as a painkiller. Unfortunately, it is also has a number of side-effects, including respiratory failure, coma and death. In addition, heroin is highly addictive, and prolonged use is associated with increased tolerance, which means that higher dosages are required to attain the same effects.

LSD (Lysergic acid diethylamide)

Topic	Response
Action	Not properly understood. We know that LSD binds to dopamine and serotonin receptors in the brain. It seems most likely that its effects are related to its ability to mimic the action of serotonin. We also know that the cerebral cortex and locus ceruleus are the regions of the brain most affected by its action.
Effect	Unpredictable. Includes: hallucinations, intensified sensory experiences, heightened awareness, euphoria, fear, anxiety, paranoia, mood swings, psychosis, increased blood pressure, sweating, and tremors.

Nicotine

Topic	Response
Action	It takes about seven seconds for nicotine to get from the bloodstream into the brain. In the brain, it binds to the nicotinic acetylcholine receptors, with the effect of increasing the production of epinephrine, norepinephrine, and dopamine.
Effect	Nicotine is a stimulant. It increases heart rate, blood pressure, concentration, and learning. It can produce mild states of euphoria. It is associated with appetite suppression, and therefore weight loss.

Unconsciousness

Most comas are induced by system-wide damage as a result of a brain trauma. The Glasgow Coma Scale measures the depth of a coma using three tests. The scores are added together and the higher you score the less severe the coma. A score of three indicates the deepest level of unconsciousness, a score of fifteen means you're fully awake.

Glasgow Coma Scale

Test Points	Eyes	Verbal	Motor
6	N/A	N/A	Obeys commands
5	N/A	Oriented, converses normally	Localizes painful stimuli
4	Opens eyes spontaneously	Confused, disoriented	Flexion/withdrawal to painful stimuli
3	Opens eyes in response to voice	Utters inappropriate words	Abnormal flexion to painful stimuli
2	Opens eyes in response to painful stimuli	Incomprehensible sounds	Extension to painful stimuli
1	Does not open eyes	Makes no sounds	Makes no movements

The longer you've been in a coma, and the greater its depth, the less likely it is that you'll wake up. The curious thing about a persistent vegetative state (PVS), the almost complete absence of brain activity in the cortex, is that the lower-level structures of the brain, such as the brainstem, remain relatively intact, so patients might open their eyes, moan, or grind their teeth, even though they are not concsious.

The deepest level of unconsciousness is brain death, where the brain has simply ceased to function. There is no response to any form of stimulation, just a flat EEG. It marks the finish of one instantiation of evolution's greatest achievement, the organ that has raised human beings up above the rest of the natural world – the brain.

Bibliography

Books

Finger, Stanley, *Minds Behind the Brain - A History of the Pioneers and Their Discoveries,* (Oxford University Press, 2000)

Clark, Mary E, *In Search of Human Nature,* (Routledge, 2002)

Forgas, Joseph P. (ed.), *Handbook of Affect and Social Cognition,* (Lawrence Erlbaum Associates, 2001)

Gibb, Barry J, *The Rough Guide to the Brain,* (Rough Guides, 2007)

Gellatly, Angus and Zarate, Oscar, *Introducing Mind and Brain,* (Totem Books, 2003)

Nolte, John, *The Human Brain: An Introduction to its Functional Anatomy,* (Mosby, 2002)

Gleitman, Henry, *Psychology (7th Edition),* (W. H. Norton, 2007)

Bear, Mark F, Connors, Barry and Paradiso, Michael, *Neuroscience: Exploring the Brain (3rd Edition),* (Lippincott Williams and Wilkins, 2006)

Websites

Neuroscience for Kids: faculty.washington.edu/chudler/neurok.html

Know Your Brain: www.ninds.nih.gov/disorders/brain_basics/know_your_brain.htm

IQ Test Questions – The Answers (from page 67)

1. Shape 3.

   EXPLANATION: The center shape in each column and row – i.e., it works horizontally and vertically – is made out of the other two shapes in each column or row, except that the circle is eradicated if it is duplicated.

2. (c). 48 minutes.

3. (d). Peleus

   EXPLANATION: Greek mythology is the key here – Priam was the father of Paris; Peleus is the father of Achilles. (You don't need to know the name of Achilles' father to get this right, you just need to know that Peleus isn't a city!)

Index

Picture Credits

The publishers would like to thank the following for permission to
    reproduce images:

Richard Burgess: pp. 11, 15, 19, 42, 46, 47, 65, 72, 89, 118;
Center of Neuro Skills: p. 13;
Dreamstime: p. 45;
Getty Images: pp. 110, 116;
Richard Haier: p. 70;
Istock: pp. 7, 26, 35, 39, 40, 80, 82, 107;
Photolibrary: p. 76;
Diana Reiss: p. 113;
Science Photo Library: pp. 8, 28, 30, 33, 36, 55, 57, 84, 98;
Paul Thompson/UCLA School of Medicine: p. 52;
University of Wisconsin-Madison (USA) Comparative Mammalian
    Brain Collections, Wally Welker, Curator; www.brainmuseum.org,
    with support from the US National Science Foundation: p. 51